SAY GOODBYE TO YOUR SMALLNESS SAY HELLO TO YOUR GREATNESS

Ida Greene, Ph.D.

SAY GOODBYE
TO YOUR SMALLNESS
SAY HELLO
TO YOUR GREATNESS

Ida Greene, Ph.D.

Acknowledgements

This book is the culmination of the ten years I spent conducting self-esteem, personal growth workshops and seminars. Everything we do is for our healing. And my self-esteem was in need of repair, when I came out of an abusive marriage.

I had to work through the emotional trauma of physical abuse, and overcome the embarrassment of being a highly educated woman who allowed herself to be abused. I like myself now as well as others. I know my feelings are important and that I matter. I pray that persons who read this book understand how valuable they are to life. The contribution you make to the world may seem small, but it is who you are. You are you and that is enough. You matter, you count, the world would be incomplete without you and your gift.

Meditate daily to discover your purpose for living and why you exist. You are here by a divine plan, and whether you understand it or not, the universe is unfolding as it should.

Ida Greene

Foreword

This book is about the struggles of life we needlessly encounter, because we do not fully understand what life and living is about. I have come to agree with Buddha, that pain is necessary in life, but that struggle is optional. What he is saying to us, is that it is not what happens to us in life that affects us, but it is the expectations and the beliefs that we hold about what happens to us, that will determine how we feel and respond to the circumstances of life.

Life is not fair, and it is not just. It is a proving ground and training camp for us to work out our soul's salvation. Due to a lot of soul searching and studying about the meaning of life, I have come to the conclusion that there is such a thing as reincarnation. I am certain that I have lived before, because of the situations and experiences I have encountered in this lifetime. The only value that the concept of reincarnation serves is the idea of a cause and an effect. I am certain that much of my pain and suffering in this lifetime is because of past erroneous beliefs and ideas that I have embraced. I have endured so much pain and suffering in my life that I do not want to go through this experience called life again. I certainly do not believe in suicide, for I believe it is an unpardonable sin.

I see that the only purpose for us to be in a body or to cope with the pain of life is to perfect our soul. The only way a diamond can be perfected is for it to go through a refining process. Likewise the only way to get a perfect pearl is through roughness and friction. And the only way you and I can perfect our soul is to become like the Christ. We must die daily to our old nature. We humans are creatures of comfort and familiarity. We resist change and we hate change. Yet, this is the only way we can grow. We want to hang on to our old ways, old beliefs, old behavior patterns, and old life styles. Even though they may have never worked, or may have caused us much pain and suffering. We tell ourselves, some crazy things like, "Bad love is better than no love at all, it is better to stick with what you know, than to try something you don't know, (even if it is detrimental or life threatening)." One in the basket is better than two in the bushel." I understand this person, at least I know what this person will do, (do you really? Do you know what you will do in every situation?)," I don't want to start all over again; This is hard; Life is hard; "If this is going to be like this forever, I want to just end it all, I can't take this anymore, I am just ready to go meet my maker." All of these are statements we have said to ourselves at one time or another.

We are children of God. We were made in the image and likeness of God, and we have the properties of God, which is to create. We are creative beings; therefore everything we speak is created through the power of our spoken word. There is power in the spoken word. God spoke and the world was created. Likewise, when we speak, good or bad is manifested. The power in the universe is creative, and IT only knows how to create. So be careful of what you think, because every thought we think is like a prayer being uttered to God. God loves us very much; He only knows how to say yes. And HE says yes to every thing we think, or speak. Watch what you think, and pay close attention to what you say. Because GOD doesn't know the difference, between when we are serious and when we are joking. God loves us, wants us to be happy, so HE/IT gives us whatever it is we say. You might say we are co creators with God, because we only have to think the thought, or say the words, for God to know what it is we desire. Every word we speak is a prayer registered in heaven, and God answers all prayers. Some prayers may be answered more quickly than others, because of the emotion, or intensity with which we speak it, but all prayers will eventually be answered. Including the one we jokingly state or seriously say like, "I just want to end it all, or I wish I could just drop dead."

Some prayers are not answered quickly because God is trying to find the right person, best combination, right outcome, or someone to say "yes," I will help this person. So many people say God can use them, however when things don't turn out to their liking, they change their mind, and God has to start looking for another way to answer your prayer, or solve your problem. Many are called, but few are chosen. Either because it is not what the person thought it would be, or they may just tell God he has the wrong person (not me this time, lord, please find somebody else). God has as much trouble getting us to do his will (through other people) as we have getting others to help us or say yes). The greatest prayer you can utter for your soul's salvation and perfection, that I had to learn is—"Yes Lord, Yes Lord, from the bottom of my heart, and the depth of my soul, Yes Lord, I now say Yes!"

It seemed to me that everything I did, came to a point where nothing was working. So I surrendered my will and just said, not my will Father, but let thy will be done in my body, mind, and soul. Then things began to work better in my life, with happier results for everyone. I had to let go and let God take over my problems.

This is why I have decided to get everything right in this lifetime, because I don't want to come back for another earth experience. I have had enough pain in this life to last me through many lifetimes. There are many milestones in life, and unfortunately we have to go through them or stagnate, die slowly, and repeat the lesson again in another lifetime. Not me, I say give me my milestones, because God and I together can handle them one by one.

Contents

Chapter 1

Self-Esteem—The Foundation of You

Our self-esteem is a blue print of who we are, how we have been treated, respected, appreciated and identified by those around us, and our external family. Our self-image is a by-product of our self-esteem. It reflects how we picture our self; how we honor, respect, and value our self. It paints a mental picture from our inner belief, of whom we think we can be, or what we believe we can do in life.

Our self-esteem is the vehicle we use to move through life to achieve a goal. It is the package we create to do the things we need to do or reach the goals we set for ourselves. Each person has a separate agenda, which is determined by what they have been called to do in this lifetime. If our self-esteem is wholesome and we feel good about our self, we can accomplish great things. If our self-esteem is damaged, or less than what it could be, our ability to accomplish or achieve will be hampered by a negative self-concept, which creates a self-image that tells us we are less than others, not good enough, that we cannot, or will not be successful in life.

The irony of this twisted thinking is that we are each marching to a different drummer. God does not repeat itself in any two persons even in identical twins. Each person is unique and different. There are no two people alike. God is faceless, colorless, sexless, loving, kind, wise, compassionate, and understanding. God is referred to as the Tao in Buddhism. Many call God "Jehovah". Whatever you call God, God is Omnipotent, All Powerful, Omnipresence, everywhere, Omniscience, All Knowing and Above All.

Try to picture God as your BIG mom, dad, brother, sister, relative, friend, helper, playmate, or the many roles people play in your life. I refer to God as "IT," this way I do not confuse the actions or works of God with those of people.

1

God has magic and can do what people cannot do. God has no limitations. Because God is God, there is nothing God cannot do. God is the "I AM." So be careful what you attach to the words "I AM." God is All Powerful. God is everywhere. God is in everyone, and in everything, including the storm, lightning, and thunder. This is how God purifies the earth to make it safe for us to breathe clean air. God has ITS own way and time to do things. You will never figure out the "whys" of life, so don't drive yourself mad or waste your time. God is God, therefore God has to answer to no one, and does not tell anyone what God has planned or how God will proceed.

We are created by the same God; one piece of cookie dough but many varieties of cookies. Some pinkish white, dark chocolate brown, (like African Americans), brown, yellow, and olive toned. All are related, and all belong to God. All things created by God have a life cycle. All are born, developed, created, and all change, disappear and die. Nothing is static. All is in motion, continuous energy transformation. This is why it does us no good to hold on to the experiences of yesterday. Yesterday, as good as it was, is gone. It will never be repeated. Try as you may, it will never come back. This is the way God planned the world. You can get angry, curse God or shake your fist at God; God does not care. But you will never be able to control God. This is my one gem of wisdom I discovered about life. You can try through trial and error to discover that God is Omnipotent "All Powerful," Omnipresence "Everywhere," Omniscience "In Every Thing." We are one with all life and one with God. We are the daughters and sons of God. Because God loves us, He has given us an earth mother, father, and family to care for us. Some do a great job, and others do a lousy job. It matters not, because God eventually returns His children to Himself, through the death experience.

What God does for us is determined by our relationship with Him. If you trust God, have unshakable faith, and love God with all your soul, and with all your mind and body, you will achieve greatness. However if you rely only on your human ego which, is fallible, you will endure needless pain and suffering.

We see God through our inner eye, the imagination. So each person will see, and experience God differently according to their perception of God and experiences of life. If the image we have of ourselves is negative or distorted it will affect how well we do in life, and how we react to our life experiences.

A negative self-image reminds us continually that we can not or may not measure up to the standards of society. It matters not whether this is a fact or fiction, if it is believed by anyone person or member of a given race it will hamper greatly the contribution the individual makes in life because they will be looking through a set of distorted glasses that says to them, "I am different from others and I am not O.K." Depending on our self-concept/self-image, self-respect, and self-esteem, we will rise to great heights or fall to the depths of despair.

Studies have shown that girls have lower self-esteem than boys. Advertising and society's idea of how girls should look and behave are blamed for them focusing their attention on appearance and a quiet demeanor rather than on their abilities.

All human beings need the following:
1. Security—Self-Acceptance, a sense of belonging to Someone/something
2. Identity—Self-Concept
3. Support—Mental, Physical and Emotional
4. Desire—Dream/Vision/Goal
5. Self-Esteem—Internal belief about yourself and the way you experience life. The parts or aspects of your self-esteem are self-concept, self-image, self-respect, self-worth, and self-confidence.
   A. Self-Concept-Personal and Spiritual Identity
   B. Self-Image—Inner picture of how you see yourself, reflected outside you.
   C. Self-Respect—Positive self-regard
   D. Self-Worth—Importance to family, society, life (God)

      E.   Self-Confidence—Self-assured, comfort, an inner peace
6.   Spirituality—Your anchor, purpose for living, to contribute, make a difference.
7.   Esthetics Appreciation—non-human, sense of awe and majesty.

We develop a **Sense of Security** by having our birth, and existence validated by someone other than our self. Someone who by their words, actions and deed say "I am glad you were born." If you get this message from a core family member, it adds to your self-worth, and self-acceptance. This helps to create feelings of belonging, and importance.

A positive **Identity/Self-Concept** enables you to accept yourself, in spite of shortcomings or perceived deficiencies. If you acknowledge yourself as a work of art, a masterpiece evolving; you accept yourself at your current level of growth, with the capacity to improve, and become better. And you are aware that your self-concept is not one, but two-dimensional. You have a Personal Self-Concept Identity and a Spiritual Self-Concept/Identity. Your self-image (inner self-picture) is formed based on the concept you have of yourself.

Your Identity is the core aspect of you. I refer to it as the Self-Concept. Because of it there are no two people alike. God created everyone different and unique. Therefore you are special, one of a kind. You are as different from every one in the universe as an apple is to an orange. There is no comparison between the two. God has built within each person a spiritual yardstick to which we all must grow before we die. Each lesson is equally challenging and hard for each person. We decide with God before we come to earth the best conditions (parents, race, sex, country) to help us grow and blossom spiritually. The human experience is a refining process necessary for our soul to evolve and develop.

God allows us to decide the particulars of how we want to live our life and what we want to do or accomplish. Some of us decide to come to earth to give joy to parents for a day, a year, seven years or seventy years. Whatever we do with our life, it must be a masterpiece for God to behold. From God we come, and to God we return after our brief journey on earth. And since no one knows when the final hour will be to return to God, it is best that we make each day count.

You must do your best daily to be the best person you can be. Sometimes you do not get a second chance to clear up a destructive or unproductive life. It is easy to look at another person and wish you were them. Yet you do not know the painful trials they endure as they smile. Remember, you were chosen to live this lifetime. You said yes to God and to life. God never promised any of us that we would live a life free of hardship or challenge. Life is an unpainted canvas. You can create as many scenes as you like. Life is a journey, not a destination. When you stop growing you slowly die. So pause if you must. Take time to enjoy the scenery and the stage production you create. For what you are is Gods' gift to you. What you make of yourself is your gift to God. When you die and leave the planet will you leave God a masterpiece of your life experiences, or give back the heap of ashes from whence you came. Your self-identity is beautiful, and magnificent. You are one of a kind, a rare gem. Your self-concept is the basic foundation of you. To be the person God designed you to be requires you to develop both your Personal and Spiritual Self-Concept. Most of us spend little time on developing our Spiritual Self-Concept. It is just as important a part of you as your Personal Self-Concept. Both aspects of your nature need to be cultivated and developed.

Support—Mental, Physical, Emotional Body—We achieve maturity and grow spiritually by working through our inner support system; our mental, physical, and emotional bodies. We have an internal drive to achieve, excel, and be a better person. To gain mastery over our lower nature and achieve perfection, spiritually, we were given a physical body to work through our character imperfections, to help us rise from our lower self to our higher self. Your task is to seek ways to improve the mental, physical and emotional aspects of yourself. This will provide the self-discipline you need to complete your primary task in life, which is soul perfection.

Desire/Dream/Goals—Belief in yourself, to know you are valuable to life. Like yourself enough to have goals and be willing to take risks, or plan how you will live your life. The ability to dream or envision goals is God's divine plan to inspire us to reach and stretch beyond our human limitations. Most big goals and some little goals require us to partner with God for their completion and success. Dreams are the longings God placed inside us to help us maintain our connection to Him. You may choose to interchange the word "It" for God, if it helps to understand the dual nature of God, who is both impersonal and personal. God does not possess the human attributes of anger, jealousy, envy and revenge. However, you may at times see humans display attributes of God.

The attributes of God are: **Love (unconditional), Empathy, Peace, Harmony, Joy, Kindness, Compassion, Tranquility, Gentleness, Consolation, Understanding, Excellence, and Creativity.**

Self-Esteem—The way you act is a measure of your self-esteem. Although our self-concept has many intricate parts, our self-esteem is composed of many selves. Your self-concept is one of the many selves of your self-esteem. They are the morals and values of your individual and cultural identities. The way you think and feel about yourself, and your relationship to others. Webster's dictionary defines it as "A confidence and satisfaction in oneself. The California State Task Force on Self-Esteem defines it as "Appreciating my own worth, and importance, and having the character to be accountable for myself, and act responsibly towards others. The parts or aspects of your self-esteem are self-concept, self-image, self-respect, self-worth, and self-confidence.

Key Elements Of Your Self-Esteem

Self-Esteem = a) Self-Concept/Identity → Cultural Morals,

values, Ethnic Pride, sense of belonging, b) Self-Image →
Cultural Self-Image → Spiritual Self-Concept/Identity, c) Self-
Respect, d) Self-Worth, e) Self-Confidence
Self-Esteem—Morals and values of your individual and cul-
tural identities.

A.   **Self-Concept/Self Identity**—Your self-identity has
three selves:
1.   **Personal Self-Identity** is composed of your cultural morals, values, and ethnic pride. It is formed
by cultural mores and values of elders
2.   **Societal/Social Self-Identity**—Is the active or
doing part of you. It is a sense of belonging to
someone or something.
3.   **Spiritual Self-Identity**—is the being part of you,
God is this part. God is experienced through your
faith; your acceptance or belief in a Supreme
Power. (Or when you have a strong knowing, that
what you desire God will grant, if it is wholesome, for the good of all, and does not harm anyone.

B.   **Self-Image**—The self you show the world.
The self-image evolves continually, according to the
situations and experiences you encounter. It is fragile;
can be distorted, damaged, or enhanced. Your environment and the people with whom you associate determine how you see yourself. If you associate with
priests, you may see yourself as a holy person. If you
associate with a gang, you may see yourself as a gang
member, (Blood, Cript, Skinhead).
a.   **Cultural Self-Image**—The picture you create of
self based on internalized beliefs, seen outside
you as behavior.

C.   **Self-Worth**—Everyone is worthy to be alive. You are
worthy to be alive or God would not have created you.
It may be that you are seeing yourself from a distorted
negative view that needs to be updated. No one is all

bad. To increase your self-worth, identify positive traits or characteristics that set you apart from others. Ask an elderly person, religious figure or anyone who has an unbiased opinion of you this question. We all do things sometimes that make us feel ashamed. However we can ask God to forgive us and avoid doing the given behavior again.

D. **Self-Respect**—To like yourself, have a high opinion of yourself as equal to others. If you have little or no respect for the feelings of others, it is because you have been hurt by someone in the past and still feel the emotional pain. . It is the nature of all human beings to be caring and kind. However if you have been treated in an unloving, unkind manner you will become bitter, and develop a hard exterior. Because you are afraid you may get hurt again. Another of my mother's African sayings is, "A burnt child fears fire".

When unpleasant things happen to us, it makes us afraid to trust. For we fear the same thing will happen again. You must respect yourself enough to want to behave, and get along with others. As a child if you were in trouble at home, or school, the only image people will have of you is the bad image you have shown. You can create a new image any time you desire. However it will require you to change. Most people are too lazy, or fear change so they remain the same. We can become comfortable with a bad self-image/concept, or a good one.

E. **Self-Confidence**—To have courage, self-assured without fear, willing to take risks. There are five types of persons will destroy your belief in self. They are Bullies, Manipulators, Braggers, Critics, and Intimidator.

Factors that affect our self-confidence are:
Shame (exclusion)
Over protection/over concern
Hurtful words (hostility/blame)
Disapproval
Low expectations (little or no trust)

Your Self-Esteem can be likened to a car. It will take you where you direct it. Depending upon your level of self-worth, self-appreciation and self-image. It is the vehicle you use as you travel through life. Depending upon your attitude, you will soar to great heights or fall to the depths of despair. For you choose your attitude each day. You can create through your imagination a glass half full or one that is empty. When life gives you lemons, you can make lemonade out of it. I constantly remind myself what the Bible says about our attitude. It says the rain falls on the just and unjust alike. So if you are drinking lemons today, remember that your friends may have their lemon experiences at a different time in life than you. Just know that sometimes you may smile to keep from crying. And you will smile outwardly sometimes as you cry inwardly. Other times, the best that you can do is pray, to have faith that God will be with you as you go through your valleys of life.

You can control what you do, but you have no control over the life or affairs of others. It is your expectation of what you think should happen that will create problems for you. Lost expectations—Is when you grieve over things that didn't happen. Or hold on to things that did not happen, that will cause you to feel down in spirit, disappointed, and depressed.

When you accept things as they are, it allows room for divine intervention. Sometimes God has a better plan for us than the one we had thought best. However we need to let go a: what if, why, why didn't it, I wish it had mind-set. Learn to say "this Lord or something better." When things do not happen as you had hoped, be open to expect a miracle. A miracle can happen for you, if you are open to receive it. God cannot and will not go through a closed mind. Open your mind and heart to receive a miracle. Say silently to yourself 25 times right now. *Miracles happen every minute of the day, so I am expecting a miracle to happen for me right now.*

Life is full of valleys, and disappointing situations. So you must not despair as you go through them. Dr. Robert Schuller, at the Crystal Cathedral Church in Garden Grove CA, speaks about "Peak to Peak Experiences" in one of his books. He says to keep your attention on the Peak (wonderful) Experiences of life and you will hardly notice the valleys of life. Your self-esteem will be affected positively or negatively by the peak and valley experiences in your life. Our self-esteem is endless; it evolves continually. It is fragile and can be affected negatively by several factors.

Your self-worth, self-respect, and self-confidence can be destroyed easily by a careless remark or inconsiderate act. So they all need daily care and reinforcement. The aspect of your self-esteem you need to tend daily are your:

A. **Self-Worth**—Belief in self, to know you are valuable to life, yourself and others. See yourself as equal to all.

B. **Self-Respect**—To like yourself, hold an opinion of yourself. Your self-respect—is like a two-edge sword. It can help or hinder you. You will have to decide if the way you are presently behaving is helping you or hurting you. The crucial question to ask "is God pleased with my behavior? For this is the final test you must pass when you die. Everyone will need to make an assessment for what they did or did not do with their life. If you are an atheist or agnostic, and do not believe in God; know that your ego, personality, and physical body will die. You will not live forever, and you will go some place when you leave planet earth. Based on your deeds you may return to the dust, from whence you came, or soar among the heavenly bodies. Have you decided what you want as the final outcome when you die? Life is precious, respect it. It is not yours to give or take away.

C. **Self-Confidence**—Courage, self-belief without fear, able to take risks. There are three types of personalities that tend to destroy your belief in self. They are bullies, manipulators, and braggers. To raise your self-confidence, write things you do well, or others say you do well.

  a.

  b.

  c.

D. **Self-Image**—The self-image evolves continually, according to the situations, and experiences you encounter. It is the inner, picture of how you see yourself, reflected in your behavior. We see from the inside out, so we may not always have an accurate picture of who we are. If any of the parts that formulate our self-image is distorted, our self-image will be distorted.

Persons with a high self-esteem know they have a right to have the following...Place a check mark by the ones you know you deserve

They have the right to:
  Respect
  Dignity
  Esteem (to be esteemed)
  Be appreciated
  Empathy
  Shared sentiments
  Be addressed with kind words
  Be given accurate information
  Be open, have two-way communication
  For people to give them their full attention
  Be cared for
  Feel a sense of equality

Our self-esteem is fragile. It can be affected by many things. Listed above are factors I have noticed in my counseling practice that affected the self-esteem of my clients. Select from the list, anything you feel has affected your self-esteem. Write why this has occurred in the space provided.

There are many things that affect the person we are, and the person (face) we present to the world. Are you aware there are many parts that make the whole of you? You are composed of many thoughts, feelings, beliefs, attitudes, emotions, wishes, longings, limitations, disappointments, setbacks, dreams, hopes, and aspirations. Can you think of things you do well?
<u>I Am Good At Doing The Following</u>:

A.

B.

C.

Factors That Impact Our Self-Esteem are:
1. Cultural Values of Acceptable, Appropriate Behaviors.
2. Ridicule/Embarrassment → Shame → Low Sense of Self
3. Self Limiting Beliefs → Thoughts → Behavior
4. Amount of Energy and Attachment to Be, Do, Act Out any of the above

   Culture → Identity→ Ethnic Pride → Acculturation
   Assimilation → Integration

Identify which of the above category/ies has had an effect on your self-esteem. <u>State below how this has influenced your personal and professional life.</u>

Spiritual Self-Concept—Our spiritual connection to a Supreme Being gives us a sense of being part of a larger group, the family of mankind. Which acknowledges our relationship to all humanity. If you get a sense of your connection to the family of mankind you can travel around the world, and feel assured you would receive kindness from others. It is only when you are fearful, have feelings of superiority, feel unrelated to people around you, or feel isolated, that you are a stranger. Spiritually we are all related. Our true parents are our heavenly Father/Mother not our earthly mother and father. Our true country is the Kingdom of heaven where God lives inside us.

Esthetics Appreciation This allows you to connect with the non human world of nature—the ocean, waterfall, star, sun, moon, sky, tree, art, sculpture, drama, play, music, a song, bird, and airplane are all works of beauty. God, our Higher Power, Supreme Being, allows us to have a larger view of the world, to see our connection to the world. Everyone has value, and is valuable, including you. The Vision of Enoch says this.

GOD SPEAKS TO MANKIND

I speak to you.
Be still, know that I am God.

I spoke to you when you were born
Be still, know that I am God.

I spoke to you at your first sight.
Be still, know that I am God.

I spoke to you at your first word.
Be still, know that I am God.

I spoke to you at your first thought.
Be still, know that I am God.

I speak to you through the dew of the morning.
Be still, know that I am God.

I speak to you through the peace of the evening.
Be still, know that I am God.

I speak to you through the storm and the clouds
Be still, know that I am God.

I speak to you through the grass of the meadows.
Be still, know that I am God.

I speak to you through the trees of the forest.
Be still, know that I am God.

I speak to you through the valleys and the hills.
Be still, know that I am God.

I speak to you Through the Holy Mountains.
Be still, know that I am God.

I speak to you Through the rain and the snow.
Be still, know that I am God.

I speak to you Through the waves of the sea.
Be still, know that I am God.

I speak to you Through the splendor of the sun.
Be still, know that I am God.

I speak to you Through the brilliant stars.
Be still, know that I am God.

I speak to you When you are alone.
Be still, know that I am God.

> —THE ESSENE GOSPEL OF PEACE—BOOK TWO

The Primary Factors That Shape Our Self-Esteem

As you go through this list, place a (+) or (-) by any category that evokes a positive or negative reaction in you and state why, underneath each section.

1. Parental readiness and acceptance—Rejection, non-acceptance by parents

2. Sex of child

3. Cultural concept of beauty
   (skin color, hair texture, nose structure etc.)

4. Physical and emotional health of mother

5. Physical health of infant (physical deformity or abnormality)

6. Cultural customs, folklore, beliefs, ethnic identity and pride

7. Expectations—what you need to do, or say to be a family member. What you are seen as capable to **do** or **be**. What your mom and dad expects of you. what you expect of yourself. Holding on to things that did not happen will cause you to feel down in spirit, disappointed, and depressed.

8 Inadequate support system for bonding (grandparent, aunt, uncle).
   A. Do you Have a substitute for an inadequate family member/s? Example, A play mom (someone you ask to play the role of your biological mom,

because she is unable, an alcoholic or drug user) i.e. God mother/dad.

B.   Who is/was the person? Whose role are/did they take your dad or mom?

C.   Does/did any older family member single you out for attention? Was this good or bad?

D.   Is there any family member you dislike/d? Why?

Secondary Factors That Negatively Affect Your Self-Esteem

1.   Be Different—Or treated different by others.
2.   Shame—Feel shy, self conscious (body deformity, thin, fat, short, tall, dark skinned)
3.   Rejection—Low self-approval/non acceptance by others, no affection.
4.   Ridicule—Set apart from others or embarrass, laughed at, made fun of.
5.   Fear/Intimidation—Worry, anxiety about a real or imagined harm.
6.   Self-Doubt—What you think you can or can't do, uncertainty.
7.   Low Self-Respect—Behave or dress in a distasteful way, speak to a degrading way. Use negative words to describe self (nigger, blood).
8.   "Something for Nothing" mind set—Allows one to be tricked, misled.

9. Criticism—Unjust, unkind words, disapproval, judge self and others.
10. Lack of Self-Discipline over mouth, self-interest, anti-social behavior.
11. Intolerance/Impatience—Anxious, nervous, quick to anger or easily offended.
12. Lack of Affection—Caring, inability to feel or express self.
13. Insecurity—Inability to trust self or others, need to be perfect or right.
14. Lack of Encouragement or Praise—To put down, or have low expectations for.
15. Low Self-Appreciation—Unsure of oneself, allow others to disrespect you.
16. Assimilate—Integrate into a group/culture that does not accept you.
17. Poor Listening Skills—Inability to hear new information and act or not act.
18. Rebellion—Willful, refusal or inability to cooperate.

Which factor/s above has influenced your self-esteem?
State why below.

1.

2.

3.

4.

Descriptive Words To Better Understand Yourself
Describe a time when you felt each of the emotions listed
below:

1. I felt FRUSTRATED when

2. I felt LONELY when

3. I felt EXCITED when

4. I felt NERVOUS when

5. I felt SCARED when

6. I felt ANGRY when

7. I felt SORRY when

8. I felt DISAPPOINTED when

ALWAYS LIVE LIFE TO THE FULLEST
A Guide to Self-Esteem

Don't let go of hope. Hope gives you the strength to keep
going When you feel like giving up. Don't ever quit
believing in yourself.
As long as you believe you can, you will have a reason for
trying.
Don't let anyone hold your happiness in their hands;
hold it in yours, so it will always be within your reach.
Don't measure success or failure by material wealth,
but by how you feel; our feelings determine the richness of
our lives.
Don't let bad moments overcome you; we all need it from time
to time.
Don't run away from love but towards love, because it is our
deepest joy.
Don't wait for what you want to come to you. Go after it with
all that you are, knowing that life will meet you halfway.
Don't feel like you've lost when plans and dreams fall short of
your hopes.
Anytime you learn something new about yourself or about life,
you have progressed.
Don't do anything that takes away from your self-respect.
Feeling good about yourself is essential to feeling good
about life.
Don't ever forget how to laugh or be too proud to cry.
It is by doing both that we live life to its fullest.
—NANCYE SIMS

ON ANGER

They learn that those who lose their temper, lose. That if you
have a sense of humor you will be unstoppable.
—ANON

20

Chapter 2

The Beginning Of You—The Self-Concept

Personal Self-Concept→ a) Expressive b) Creative → Societal
(Public) Social Self-Concept → Spiritual Self-Concept →

Your self-concept has three selves.1) Personal Self-Identity,
2) Societal/Social Self, 3). Spiritual Self-Concept.

1. **Personal Self-Concept** a) Expressive Self, it is your ability to provide for your self, your money making ability.,
   b) Creative Self reflects your personal growth, and is
   expressed through your desire for success, or to achieve. It
   is your tendency to create your ideal self, your undiscov-
   ered inner self and talents.
2. **Societal/Social Self-Concept**—focuses on relationships
   and interpersonal relationships.
3. **Spiritual Self-Concept**—The part of us that connects to a
   Supreme Deity. It is an inner essence that is waiting to
   burst forth. It creates your daily circumstances through
   your thoughts, beliefs, and visions.

Your Personal Self-Concept
Usually your Personal Self-Concept focuses on power. How
much you have or can exercise. We do not have power. We
merely use the power in the universe for either good or bad.
Power is how you express yourself and view your relationship
to the Universal Power/God. Ask yourself if you believe there is
a Supreme power that rules the earth, or do you see yourself as
the ultimate power in the universe? If you say yes, that places a
tremendous burden on you to control everything, and little time
to enjoy life. Also if you are the ultimate power you should be
able to keep everyone alive forever including yourself. If you
are the ultimate power, then you can decide when day will end,

and nighttime begins. You also decide when it will rain, snow, thunder, whether the day will be cloudy or sunshine. Isn't it wonderful to be a child of God, so you do not have to worry about these things. Always remember that as a child of God, you are the little "I," not the "Big I." You are the image of God, the "little God," not the "Big God."

It is important to understand your relationship to God. You are a child of God, therefore whatever you need, you merely ask and divine ideas will come to you as what you need to do to have your needs met. God will supply you with the wisdom to get your needs met. Also, you were given an earth (human) mother and father, to care for you, and look after your needs. Sometimes they turn out to not be the best.

Love is the one emotion that can keep you sane, and centered in what often appears to be an insane world. Love can see you through the most difficult times and support you in the midst of the most demanding challenges. You can move beyond any fear caused by human differences whether it be differences in race, creed, choice of lifestyle, national culture, or difference of opinion.

Through love you can overcome fear of illness, lack, or any other condition that causes you concern. This is here your faith and belief that God has heard your prayer, is critical. God hears your prayers, and answers in <u>God's own time</u>, not your time. Because your time may not produce the best outcome. Always remember that God can see further up the road through Its spiritual eyes, than you can see with your limited human eyes.

Write below three attitudes or behaviors you dislike about yourself. Then put a check mark by the ones you would most like to change. State three things you can do to change the trait.

1.

2.

3.

Development of The Personal Self-Concept
The Foundation Of Your Self-Esteem

Self-Esteem = Personal Self-Concept → Cultural-Identity (morals, values) → Ethnic Pride creates sense of belonging → Societal Self-Concept → Personal Self-Image → Spiritual Self-Concept.

Your **Personal-Identity** (Self-Concept) is the private you that may be at odds with the values and mores of your family. For example, on my fathers' side of the family (Albert Green), "The Greens' do not believe in divorce, they try to work things out, or place them in the hands of the Lord. I was reprimanded when I decided to divorce my husband. Even though fornication was a legitimate biblical reason. Your self-concept is the imprint given to you by your family. Sometimes we inherit a distorted self-concept because the behavior, and attitude we show is seen as acceptable, however it is not acceptable to society, or to one's culture. An example would be, to tell someone a lie, because you are afraid to hurt their feelings.

Did you ever think about the concept you hold of yourself? It is an inner mental picture. Stop what you are doing now, and draw your self-concept. Draw it with your non-dominant hand in the space below (your left hand if you are right handed).

Cultural Identity/Self-Concept—One's identity as a member of a culture, or clan helps to formulate the self-concept. It is a point of reference about who one is and where they came from. Most cultures have a set of values of acceptable or appropriate behaviors one is expected to display. Sometime one's cultural values may differ from the larger societal values and cause confusion or conflict for an individual. For example if one's cultural values says it is o.k. to steal as long as you do not get caught. And the larger societal values say stealing is never acceptable behavior, the discrepancy can cause confusion and uncertainty as how one should behave, because the way people see themselves differs with how society sees them. Your cultural self-identity provides morals and values, and acts as a guideline for what is acceptable conduct and manners.

Ethnic Pride—is an important element provided by one's cultural group. It gives one a sense of belonging, and acts as a point of reference. It gives distinction, or can be a source of embarrassment and disgrace. There are family celebrations such as yearly family reunions that enhance ethnic pride.

Write below your cultural values of unacceptable behavior:

1.
2.
3.

List some ethnic values of your family/clan below:

1.
2.
3.

a. Write the values your family or culture of origin feel is acceptable below:

Finish This Sentence—I Am Special Because...

A.

B.

C.

Our culture gives us information about our ancestors, family members who lived before us. Our culture helps us create a point of reference as the beginning of our self. It provides an identity for us of how those who look like us began. It gives us a map to follow. And shows us how to begin. When the child is young, it seeks a point of reference as the beginning of self: Where did I come from? To whom do I belong? How did I get to earth? Are there other people who look like me? Our cultural ethnic identity answers this question. In the space below fill in the blanks with the appropriate information about your family tree.

My name...
Sex M/F ....

My birth date ....
Birth weight...

My birth place..
Time of birth ....

Number of brothers........Names...

....

....

Number of sisters ....Names...

....

....

My favorite food/s ....

My favorite color/s ....

My favorite animal/pet...

My Father's name...

His birth date ....

Birth weight ....

His birth place ....

Time of birth...

Things I remember my father saying to me ....

....

....

Mother's name (married)...

(maiden)..

Her birth date...

Birth weight ....

Her birth place ....

Time of birth...

Things I remember her saying to me.......................................

....

....

Father's Mother's (My Grandmother's**) name** ....
....
Her birth date ....
Birth weight ....

Her birth place ....
Time of birth ....

Things I remember her saying to me.....................................
....

....

Father's Father's (My Grandfather's**) name**...........................

His birth date ....
Birth weight..

His birth place ....
Time of birth...

Things I remember him saying to me......................................

....

....

Mother's Mother's (My Grandmother's**) name**.......................
....
Her birth date ....
Birth weight...

Her birth place...

Time of birth ....

Things I remember her saying to me...

....

....

Mother's Father's (My Grandfather's**) name** ....

....

His birth date..

Birth weight ....

His birth place...

Time of birth ....

Things I remember him saying to me...

....

....

Write any thoughts or feelings you have about your core family members. Who has contributed positively to your self-esteem and self-confidence and why?

Societal (Public) Self-Concept—Your People Skills, ability to interact effectively with others. The part of you that does what is socially acceptable. Your school and work culture reflects this self. If you are not accepted as a part of the culture where you are, you will experience confusion, feel detached, disorganized and have a sense of uneasiness until you know why you are rejected. Once you know the reason/s for your non-acceptance, you need to decide if you can handle the social isolation.

You have several options: you can become a rebel/recluse, start your own elite group, or pretend it doesn't matter while your self-image, self-esteem, and self-confidence decay as a result of the dual messages you are sending "I'm o.k./I'm not o.k./Am I really o.k.?" it is the nature of your social self to attach itself to those it identifies as societal family.

Societal, values are broad, general, and non-binding. Cultural Assimilation—means we can choose to be a part of a society, or isolate ourselves and be non-involved with the people around us. Cultural Integration is a blending into societal fabric. All cultures have behavioral do's and don'ts to guide its citizens. The American culture is Judeo Christian and follows the Ten Commandments in the Bible as a guide for how we should behave towards each other e.g. Thou shalt not kill, Thou shalt not steal etc.). However due to the separation of state and church in our government, the American society has become more government, and little or no church.

The church is the institution that provides moral training, however our society does not respect churches as in the past. The Bible for many Americans has become sports, entertainment activities, television, and Hollywood. The government was never designed to teach morality. It is not a preventative institution. It deals strictly with the law. It punishes its members after they break the law. It does not teach moral laws, the churches do that. Since the two entities can not commingle, society has to build more jails to punish people for their ignorance of moral laws or morality.

There is no Societal Self-concept. Society has no moral or

ethical guidelines for non-Christian, secular persons to follow. And no vehicle to teach or provide moral training if anyone was interested in getting it. Many people do not know that the spiritual laws of the Ten Commandments, say "Thou shalt not kill and "Thou shalt not steal." Society does not teach this, so people continue to steal and kill. Many people do not know right conduct from wrong conduct. Often when they discover this they are older than age seven, when most behavior patterns are firmly established. We always behave according to our self-concept, whether it is moral or amoral. Our social self-concept is formed from our social self-image.

Personal Self-Image—Inner picture of how you see yourself as reflected in behavior. Our social self-image is formed partly from our cultural identity through the morals, and values shared with us by elders. And the ethnic pride we develop creates a sense of belonging. From this belonging we form our self-image.

We see from the inside out, so we may not always have an accurate picture of who we are. If any part that formulates our self-image is distorted, our self-image will be distorted. An example of a distorted self-image is someone who weighs ninety pounds, but whose inner mental picture sees a fat person. To change a distorted self-image, will require you to change your self-concept. And to improve your self-esteem requires you to improve your self-concept/identity, cultural identity, ethnic pride, and self-image. There are key elements of your self-esteem that is essential for good emotional maturity. They are self-respect, self-worth, and self-confidence. Your self-image based on your self-concept.

Sometimes our self-image can be erroneous due to a false perception on our part or because someone whose opinion we value holds a negative view of us. Which may not be the truth about us. They may see us from a distorted view because we have only shown them the negative side of us. Maybe you do not see anything about yourself. If this is the case, remember you were made in the likeness of God. God created you after Itself. God is not junk and God does not make junk. If you had created yourself, you probably would have made junk. God does not see you as impossible, no good, worthless, incorrigible, a failure, or a loser. Try to see yourself through the eyes of God. See your possibilities and potential. God does not see the negative side of you.

Spiritual Self-Concept—There is a part of us that connects to a Supreme Deity, I refer to as God. We show our divinity when we are kind, considerate, compassionate, tolerant, and understanding. All of these are traits of God. God has implanted Itself within our heart, so that It can minister to us and through us to our earth brothers and sisters. However we must open our minds and our hearts, so that we are able to receive the divine inspiration, and guidance God wishes us to receive. We can all be earth angels by loving our fellow humans and behaving in a divine and angelic manner. We do this unconditional love for each other and forgiving the offenses of others seventy times seventy.

Your Spiritual Self-Concept, is the divine part of you that makes you reach out to help others. It is an expression of how you perceive (see) your self. Your Personal Self-Concept can vary from situation to situation, but not your Spiritual Self. It is the most powerful part of you. It can integrate all the other aspects of your personality (Personal Self-Concept, Social Self-Concept), however the other aspects can not. You only need to follow a few simple laws to have total dominion over the affairs of your life. They are: You shall love the Lord thy God with all thy soul, body and mind. This is a very difficult law to obey, because we make Gods out of everything and everyone. We worship the Beatles, and Tom Cruise. We swoon over and idolize Elizabeth Taylor, Elvis Presley and I am sure you can add others to this list.

The second law says we should love our neighbor as ourselves. Most of us hate and abuse ourselves, so we end up treating our neighbors with the same hate, neglect, and abuse. We abuse ourselves and others by the belittling, limiting, and self-deprecating thoughts we say silently to ourselves. Sometimes these self-deprecating thoughts are masked by arrogance, narcissism, hostility, aggression, or a sadistic attitude/behavior towards others.

In the Old Testament, the orthodox Hebrews had over 600 laws to follow daily to live a godly life. In the New Testament, the laws have been reduced to two, "Loving God and Loving your neighbor as yourself. When you love God and see yourself as a child of God it is easy to love yourself without arrogance. When you can love yourself without arrogance or self-hatred it will be easy to extend the feelings to your neighbor. For the answer to every problem you will encounter is **Love**. Love the problems you now encounter for they bring you new wisdom, growth, and maturity.

It is always wise to "love" the solution or answer you receive through divine inspiration (your hunches). It usually provides you with a blessing beyond your wildest imagination. If you see a problem or situation from a negative perspective it will be negative. If you change your view, and see a problem as an opportunity for growth, you will feel different about yourself and your relationship to the situation.

We are not isolated beings. We are a community and family of human beings, whatever affects the one, affects all. We need rules to live by to have a pleasant society. This involves self-control and self-discipline. We are a society of many cultures and traditions. Rituals such as how to treat the elderly, cultivating good manners, showing respect, mastering self-discipline, and developing self-respect identify us with our community, history, tradition, families, and culture. All cultural values are in place to help us live together in spite of our differences. Our cultural guidelines for living all have the basic principles of the Ten Commandments given to Moses by God when the earth was first formed. You will find some of your cultural do's and don'ts in the Ten Commandments. They are:

THE TEN COMMANDMENTS

1. *Thou shall have no other Gods before me. Thou shall love the Lord thy God with all thy mind, body and soul.*

2. *Thou shall love thy neighbor as thy self.*
3. *Thou shall make no graven (carved, sculptured) image of anything that is above the earth or below the sea. No idol - atry. Idolatry includes the worship of anything, as if it were independent from God.*
4. *Remember the Sabbath day to keep it holy.(Set aside one day to honor God)*
5. *Thou shall not kill. No murder.*
6. *Thou shall honor thy mother and thy father. (includes per - sons who take the place of a mom or dad).*
7. *Thou shall not use the name of the lord in vain. I swear to God, God... No blasphemy of God's name*
8. *Thou shall not commit adultery. (Lust over things that belong to your neighbor, be it a toy, car, girl friend/wife, boyfriend/husband). No adultery or incest.*
9. *Thou shall not bear false witness against thy neighbor. (Tell a lie.) Always tell the truth even if it gets you in trou - ble. It is better to be in trouble with people than with God, by breaking one of these Commandments.*
10. *Thou shall not steal. No theft.*

WORDS OF WISDOM FROM MY MOTHER ON RELATIONSHIPS
Whenever you dig a ditch for someone,
dig two, one for them and one for yourself.

You can catch more flies with honey
than you can with vinegar.

When you have your hand in a lion's mouth,
you have to ease it out slowly.

To Discover Your True Self, Ask Yourself These Questions
   1.   Who am I? <u>I am</u>:

2. Finish this Sentence "I am a product of my upbringing because…"

3. Finish this Sentence: "I am happy/ashamed of my heritage because…

4. What I really want to do in life is: write below.

6. My likes are: My dislikes are:

7. I am good at doing the following:

8. Finish this statement, "If I could only do one kind of work in life, it would be…"

9. Finish this statement, "I am most unhappy when I <u>have to</u>, need to"

10. Finish this statement, "I am the happiest when I…"

11. Finish this statement, "I am most unhappy *at work* when I have to, need to:"

12. Finish this statement, "I am the happiest *at work* when I…"

My 1-, 5-, and 10-year goals in the following areas are: write a month and year when you plan to achieve each goal.

Personal —

Professional —

Spiritual—

Social —

Chapter 3

Success—A Double Edged Sword

This chapter will help you to be clear about your mission in life, allow you to assess how far you have come and how to determine if you have the necessary traits and abilities to achieve your dreams. It will teach you how to focus and stay focused so that you can stay motivated with your chosen vision. It will help you to make sense out of all the mumble, jumble chatter in your mind. You will learn the principles of success and will be able to decide by the end of the chapter if you are a good candidate for success.

You will be given the principles of self-motivation, and what you must do on a daily basis to stay motivated. You need to be able to face the barriers (fears) that get in the way to block your vitality, allows you to become depressed, unmotivated, and procrastinate.

Do you know what barriers (fears) block your vitality, and allows you to become depressed, unmotivated, or procrastinate. Use the space below to explore your self and your life up to the present moment. Are you satisfied with who you are or who you have become? Are you ready for success?

Are You Ready for Success?
What phase of success do you need to work on at this time in your life? It is:

<u>Draw a large circle on a sheet of paper. Now create your own pie chart, showing percentages</u>.

1. Money

2. Power

3. Right Career Choice?

4. Relationships/work, family, significant othe

5. Life Style

6. Being of Service to my fellow man

7. Spiritual Values

I_____ am willing to participate in my success and will do everything within my power to be actively involved in this program of my success.

Success is a journey, the journey you travel in life until you make your transition from the planet, you are forever creat - ing and recreating anew.

Success Skills For The New Millennium

These are the skills you will need to master before you become successful. Which of these skills have you mastered? <u>Circle the ones you need to work on and state what steps you are taking or have taken to improve your deficiencies in these areas</u>:

1. Self-Esteem =

    a. Self-Concept-Identity
    b. Self-Worth
    c. Self-Respect

2. Self-Image

    a. Your strengths

    b. Your Weaknesses

    c. How you appear to others (unsure, timid)

    d. Handicaps you need to overcome

3. Self-Acceptance

    a. Self-Confidence

4. Communication Skills

5. Are You Ready for Success?

    A.   What do you want to do, be, have in:

1 year

5 years

10 years

    B. Do you have mastery in the following areas?
         If you need help, what are your plans to improve these skills?

Responsibility

Dependability

Trustworthy

Accountability

6. Things I <u>know/need</u> to favorably impress others to get my needs met are:

    a. How to dress for success-
    b. How to walk-
    c. How to talk and express myself-
    d. Interview skills I need for a job are:
    e. Knowing how to sell myself to an employer, do you know this? (Yes) (No)
    f. Writing a résumé/List the basic parts of it here:

g. Talking on the phone—telephone etiquette I need to know are, list below:

h. Marketing skills and or follow up skill I need to improve are:

7. To deal with rejection, I need to know:

a. How to accept "NO" without feeling rejected, so I will do the following:

b. I want to stay motivated during any adversity: So I will do the following:

c. I want to maintain belief in myself in hardship, disappointment, or failure, so I will do the following.

Things That Impede Or Block Success

If you can get free training in high technology or computer training, take it. You may have to start on a lower entry pay level, but the ability to advance within the corporation may be excellent.

Be willing to take a risk. *Comfort is not always growth.* You may be very comfortable in your present job environment, but how far will you have advanced in ten years? Will you be making the $70,000 you had set out to make within 10 years if that is your goal? Always maintain a competitive edge for yourself. Other skills you will need to be successful are good speaking and listening skills.

Skills For Speaking

Use "I-messages" when speaking. An I-message is a sentence that starts with the word I and expresses a feeling.

Remember to state your feelings. The four basic feelings are mad, sad, glad, and fear/afraid.

Other useful feeling words are:

- I like it when...
- I don't like it when...
- I want...
- I wish...

FACTORS THAT ENSURE OPEN COMMUNICATION

Do's and don'ts for effective listening

Don't say or imply that the person "shouldn't feel that way."

Don't express your feelings—of disagreement, when the other person is upset.

Don't interpret what you think the other person really feels.

Don't try to get the person to change their mind when they have voiced their concern or stated their position.

Do remember that every person has the right to any feeling in the world.

Do know that people do not have to agree with you or you with them for things to be O.K.

Do put your feelings "on a back burner" (lay your feelings aside) while you are the listener.

Desire for competition

You will need a strong, healthy desire for competition against yourself to move up the success ladder. There may be times when the odds are against you. However, if you have a strong belief in what you desire, it will become a reality. Remember thought follows energy, so whatever is your dominant thought will manifest through your power to create. If you think the other person feels resentful or jealous of you, it will be created through your dominant thought. Wherever the energy goes, power flows.

Your power is in your thoughts. Whatever you think about on a repetitive basis will appear in your life. So know your strengths as well as your weakness, because both will manifest through the creative power of your thoughts. As you go through this list make comments about the areas where you are weak and need to improve:

1. Self-Identity → No One to Share Burdens →Lack of Support → No Goal to Achieve → Apathy → Loss of Drive

2. Conflicting Cultural Values of Acceptable, Appropriate Behaviors.

3. Ridicule/Embarrassment → Shame → Low Sense of Self

4. Do you have negative or defeatist thoughts about yourself? If so write about it.

5. Do you have a desire to be wanted, cared about, or important to someone? Explain

6. What feelings now mask your isolation, loneliness, to compensate for companionship of the opposite sex, motherhood, or other not listed:
   a. Self Pity
   b. Anger
   c. Jealousy
   d. Resentment/Envy
   e. Revenge
   f. Pride/Self Righteousness

7. To increase your self-confidence, write things you do well or were told you did well.

1. Write the names of persons you need to forgive: Your parents, childhood caretakers, etc.

    Next to the names write:

    I now forgive you for ....

    ....

    ....

2. List negative thoughts and attitudes you have towards them:

3. Overlay your negative feelings with positive feelings about the persons listed above.

4. Sit quietly, practice, sending love to yourself and others who may have mistreated you.

5. Each day see yourself as a new born baby eager to learn, and explore newness without the fear you will make a mistake or do something wrong. Self Esteem, are you ready to change?

<u>What will you do to change the following:</u>

1. Negative beliefs about myself-

2. Negative attitude/sour disposition—

3. Accept your basic goodness-Self-Worth

To Light The Fire Within You! Avoid the 3 C's.

- Complaining—
- Criticizing—
- Condemning—

Wh at will you do?

When?

How?

How has your relationship(s) in the past impacted your interactions with others? Are you able to see your faults?

Reclaiming Your Self
1. If you have allowed others to not respect or ignore your needs and wants they will continue to do so because you allow it.
2. You must acknowledge and accept that you are important and therefore worthwhile.
3. You must have standards for yourself and your life. Let there be certain things you will not accept or tolerate.
4. Never let guilt about past wrongs get in the way of your belief that you are a worthwhile person.
5. Daily pray to God and ask his forgiveness for your wrongs.

6. Daily have a list of names of people, you ask to forgive you for past wrongs.
7. After you ask for forgiveness, do not commit the same errors (sins) again.
8. Daily forgive yourself and others for misdeeds (over).
9. Accept you are not perfect and neither is anyone else.
10. Replace your addiction to others and things with a strong love for God and doing what you know is loving, just, and the will of God.
11. Stand up for your rights. Support yourself. Say what you will and will not accept.
12. Others will respect your rights when you acknowledge and respect your rights.
13. People treat us with the same respect we feel we deserve.
14. Do not blame others if you let them violate your rights, disrespect you or ignore your wishes. You allow it because you do not take a stand.
15. Let people know that your needs are being violated. They are not mind readers.

TEN COMMANDMENTS FOR FORMERLY MARRIED

Thou Shalt Not Live In Thy Past
Thou Shalt Be Responsible For Thy Present
And Not Blame Thy Past For It.
Thou Shalt Not Feel Sorry For Thyself Indefinitely.
Thou Shalt Assume Thy End Of The Blame
For Thy Marriage Dissolution.
Thou Shalt Not Try To Reconcile Thy Past and Reconstruct
Thy Future By A Quick, New Marriage.
Thou Shalt Not Make Thy Children The Victims
Of Thy Past Marriage.
Thou Shalt Not Spend All Thy Time Trying To Convince Thy
Children How Terrible And evil Their Departed Parent Is.
Thou Shalt Learn All Thou Can About Being A One Parent
Family And Get On With It.

Thou Shalt Ask Others For Help When Thou Needest It.
Thou Shalt Ask God For The Wisdom To Bury Yesterday,
  Create Today And Plan For Tomorrow.
                    —JIM SMOKE

How To Set Boundaries For Yourself
1. Accept that you are important to life.
2. Accept that you are valued by God, therefore you have self-worth, self-value, and importance.
3. Accept that all people are special including you.
4. Respect your right to privacy as well as the rights of others.
5. Accept that no one is here to satisfy your needs and neither are you here to meet theirs.
6. Accept that others have to want to love us, and care about/care for us. We can not demand that others love us.
    It is their choice to like or love us.
7. If we have abused others either verbally, emotionally or physically they will be afraid to trust us, because they
    fear hurt by us again.
8. We have to earn others trust, love and affection, it is not
    a right or privilege they owe us.
9. Tell the truth; never say it does not matter when it does matter.
10. Accept your feelings. Acknowledge your pain, hurt, grief, sadness, disappointment, loneliness, feelings of rejection, loneliness, abandonment, depression, and feeling that no one loves you.
11 You send love to others through your thoughts, your smile, eyes and your touch. Daily send love to your-self and others.
12. Rely less on words to convey your feelings to others. Words are cheap, and useless. They do not mean any-

thing. Verbal promises are easy to break without action to back them.

13. People watch what you do, not what you say.

I ACCEPT THE RIGHT LOVE IN MY LIFE

*As I speak my word for right companionship and love,
I reaffirm my faith in Divine guidance.
I acknowledge and accept the life, and light of God's
perfect creation.
I accept the spirit within me which is already one with
the one whose love I am to share.
This spirit is attracting the two of us now, and we will
meet when the time is exactly right.
If we have already met, or if the one I am with now is in
truth the right one for me, then I shall know it, and I will
receive unmistakable guidance from my high inner Self.
I am at peace as I release this treatment into the universe.
I know that it is done. All is well with my soul.*

—ANON

How To Light The Fire Within To Succeed

Desire → Drive/Energy → Vitality →Enthusiasm →
Light/Aliveness → Fire

Our Fire Within Manifests As A Desire To Excel → Goal
→ Energy Vitality → Enthusiasm → Alive/Light →
(Joy, Happiness, Love) = FIRE

Through Our Desires and Goals We Become Motivated To Change Our Circumstances

To discover your passion in life, learn to move through your fears, and increase your self esteem. Answer these questions for yourself:

1. What things give you the greatest pleasure or satisfaction in life?

    Write them down, then prioritize in order of 1, 2, 3

Personal:

Professional:

Social:

Spiritual:

2. What things do others praise or compliment you on?

    List them below—

3. The way to know your inner self is to examine your attitudes and beliefs. What are your beliefs about life, people your family, yourself?

4. Now that you have completed the activities above, <u>what thing or things would you enjoy doing every day of the year, even if you were not paid monetarily?</u> Whatever you choose is your passion, (your hot button). To live your passion you must move through your fears and increase your self-esteem. Write about this now.

    List character flaws you have that lower your self-esteem. Which factors affect your self-esteem the most?

6. Know your strengths and weaknesses so that you empower yourself and others. Start by working on your fears (doubts, worries, apprehensions). Your fears mask both your strengths and your weakness. Your strengths are whatever other praises you on. Your weaknesses are the things you avoid doing, because of your fears whether real or imagined. Do you know what are your strengths and weakness? List them below. Both give insight into you as a person. We grow more from our weakness.

51

MY STRENGTHS   MY WEAKNESSES

Start now to enjoy the your life. *Life Is Shorter Than You Think.*

LIGHT THE FIRE WITHIN YOU

Exercises to Empower Yourself and Increase Feelings of Self-Worth

1. Write down <u>words</u> that <u>you</u> feel <u>best describe you</u>.

2. What <u>words</u> would <u>others</u> use to describe you? <u>Why</u>?

3. Are you Special? If you say no, why do you feel this way?

    State what makes you special…

4. If you could live any place in the <u>U.S., or world</u> where would you live?

5. If you could do what you wanted, what would you <u>be</u>, <u>have</u>, or <u>do</u>?

6. What do you think <u>successful people do</u> to become successful?

7. How much education do you want? Do you feel this will occur?

8. How much money do you believe you *deserve* to make/have?

9. How will you do this? List the steps you will take to make it happen.

10. Are you a Go-Getter or do you wait for things to come to you?

11. Do you want a family? How will you provide for it?

If you have a family, will you make enough money to feed, and clothe a small family of two children— $40,000 a year; or a large family, of four children— $75,000 a year?

I ACCEPT MY SELF, HEALTH, AND WEALTH

It is right, and just for me to have my needs met.
It is right and just for me to ask for and receive what I want.
It is right and acceptable by me for others to love, and show me appreciation.
I deserve love, affection, right treatment, respect and honor from others.
I am created in the image and likeness of God, and it feels good.
I am created in the image of God, who is perfection of body, mind and soul.
God cares for me and she provides for all my needs.
I do not need to ask, because my loving father, mother, God knows what I need.
I am proud to have rich, royal, wise and spiritual lineage.
All of my needs are abundantly supplied, I now cease all worry and concern so that God can perform.
I accept that I am loved beyond measure by a God who wants the best for me.
I give up all struggle and allow God to point the way.
I am patient with myself, and God as I evolve to my highest spiritual self.
I become a better human being each day, worthy to be called a child of God.
I accept all of God's creation, starting with myself.
ADAPTED BY IDA GREENE, ANON

Blocks To Your Self-Image And Self-Esteem
1. Abuse-Emotional/Physical/Verbal
2. Negative perceptions we hold about ourselves.
3. Negative perceptions others hold of us; words they use when they describe us or way they tease us, or treat us.

4. Maladaptive self-image: poor me, be perfect, klutz, superior, inferior, nag, complainer, stupid, workaholic.

    a. Which of the above masks do you wear?

    b. Can you accept yourself at your present level of being, while you seek ways to improve yourself?

5. Anger or a maladaptive expression of anger affects your self-esteem. Is this your problem, what will you do about it?

6. Using your non-dominant hand, write about your self-image.

7. Using your non-dominant hand, draw a picture of your self-image.

8. Write one word that describes your self-image.

9. What self-image would you write, if you were
    satisfied with yourself?

10. Draw a picture of this person.

Chapter 4

Manage Your Anger To
Improve Your Self-Esteem

We are all different. Even among persons of the same culture, same ethnic background, heritage and family we differ. We can see things from a different perspective because we have different thoughts, sensations, feelings, and there are different things that make us happy, sad, or disappointed. Sometimes our differences can act as a source of friction to divide rather than unite. It is these times when we need something to help us look through the same lens, so to speak, to better understand the other person. Soft Power Negotiation SkillsTM is a useful communication tool in such situations.

What Is Soft Power Negotiation Skills™?

It is understanding the self to better know how others feel, what they want/desire, and how to meet their needs to get what you want. It's the use of soft words that support and enhances you in your total expression as a person.

How Does Soft Power Negotiation Skills™ Work?

Everything we do is negotiation. All human relationships revolve around barter and exchange. Therefore all interpersonal interactions entail negotiation. Soft Power Negotiation Skills™ is the blending and interplay between your personal skills and people skills. It allows you to get what you want from others, and have them feel good about the exchange.

How Does Soft Power Differ From Hard Power?

The difference is in the way you react to others. With Hard Power, someone wants to be in control and power over the other.

HARD POWER

- Tough—Shows no compassion
- Dominant—controls, rule
- Forceful—coercion, fear
- Aggressive—verbal/physical abuse
- Attacking—confront, critical, condemns
- Intimidates—frightens, bully
- Takes what is not it's own

SOFT POWER NEGOTIATION

- Acknowledges its /others' needs
- Compassionate with self and others.
- Caring
- Self assured, deserving, self worth
- Firm, yet gentle.
- Does not seek to control, manipulate or bribe.
- Stands its ground, peacefully
- Seeks a just outcome.
- Is powerful lovingly

Anger, can be used by others to confuse or control you. In conflict resolution anger is a useful emotion when used to support yourself against attack by others. Anger takes away your energy, because it charges you emotionally, even when used constructively. Because of its potential to hurt or destroy one's self-confidence, anger must be under your control. It can be likened to an atomic bomb when uncontrolled.

Anger is a major block to your self-esteem and self-image. It is a position you choose. We decide how we will react to a perceived threat to our ego, or emotional well-being.

It is a signal to help you see what is going on in your emotions, to find the cause of the anger. Everybody has his or her own definition of anger. Webster's New World Dictionary defines anger as: a feeling of displeasure resulting from mistreatment, injury, and opposition, usually showing itself in a desire to fight back at the supposed cause of the feeling.

Anger is a valuable signal, because it lets us know when something is wrong or a problem. It does not solve the problem. **Often when we are angry, one of these things is happening**:
- We want something and are not getting it.
- From past experience, we expect trouble.
- We have feelings of powerlessness.
- Sad feelings
- Feelings of grief that connect us with strength and joy.
- Depression
- Feelings of negativity about life, self, and people.

In confronting anger, remember you have three options:
- You can choose to react angrily or not.
- You can become aware of what you are feeling.
- You can be aware of the intensity of your anger, if you are in control of your anger, or if it controls you.

Always assume responsibility for what you are feeling, and own all your feelings including anger. Anger that is unresolved turns into resentment, envy, jealousy, revenge, and hatred. Unresolved anger manifests as depression. There is always an underlying feeling of inadequacy when you are angry. Anger moves through the following stages if it is not resolved immediately: Frustration g Disappointment g Embarrassment g Guilt g Fear of Rejection.

1. Frustration—unfulfilled expectations, to prevent the occurrence of anger change your goal or plan.
2. Disappointment—unfulfilled expectations, to prevent anger, look into the situation and get the facts.
3. Embarrassment—unfulfilled self-image, desire to create a new self-image.
4. Guilt—social expectations you have accepted, decision to confront the situation, behavior, or change it.
5. Fear of rejection—unknown expectations with probability of consequence, confront the

situation/person/behavior, explore the cause then decide if you want to avoid it.

a)   Have you ever felt any of the above emotions?

b)   How do/did they make you feel about yourself?

Gender and The Expression of Anger

What we see in patterns of men who are abusive are the choices that are made. There are places and ways in which social permission is given to men and boys of when and how it is appropriate to express their anger.

There is a point where a boy has to decide "which side of the fence he is going to be on." Is he going to be on the side of the controllers or is he going to be on the side of the controlled ones? Boys often decide they are going to go with the controllers because otherwise they fear becoming gay, or they are unsure.

For a little boy to get the messages that he is gay before he knows what the words mean, say he's a sissy, more like a girl. And in our sexist culture, that means you are associated with the lesser gender, and a boy learns early in life that he needs to put a lot of energy into avoiding this association.

Anger is a waste of energy, because it takes away your joy. Anger can be used by others to confuse or control you, if you are unaware of what you are feeling, unclear about what angers you, or have no control over your angry outbursts. However, in conflict resolution, anger is a useful emotion when used to support yourself against the attack by others to over power or control you.

The premise of anger management techniques is to help you use your anger as a signal to identify your problem and deal with it. Rather than act upon your anger by lashing out, to make the situation worse, or hold your angry feelings inside.

The Major Causes of Anger Are:
- Dependency Relationships
  - Unfulfilled needs or expectations
- Resentment
- Grief
- Victim Mentality
- Abusive Relationships
- Low Self-Esteem
  - Jealousy

Anger Can Lead To:
- Angrily lashing out → makes situation worse
- Holding feelings inside → Creates resentment, and physical symptoms

OR

- You can identify the problem to handle or solve it. You do this by changing the thoughts you think. This is helpful when thinking about something that irritates you or makes you mad.

When a situation provokes you and you are preparing to respond, begin thinking, then ask yourself these critical questions.
- How can I manage this situation?

- What is it that I absolutely have to do?

- Have I decided how I will regulate my anger?

- Will an argument between me and the other person solve my problem?

- Do I have a way to get time to calm down or relax?

We define anger as a
- Physically arousing emotion, with a physiological correlate.
- A feeling, which has an effect on the way you experience your world.
- A Communicator, because it sends information to others.
- A Cause, because it produces specific effects and results.

Think about your definition of anger, write your thoughts below.

Do you understand what arouses you to anger? List below words that describe your anger:

ATTITUDE

The longer I live, the more I realize the impact of attitude on life. Attitude, to me is more important than facts. It is more important than the past, than education, than money, than cir-cumstances, than failures, than successes, than what other people think or say or do. It is more important than appear-ance, being gifted, or having special skills. It will make or break a company...a church...a home. The remarkable thing is we have a choice every day regarding the attitude we will embrace for that day. We cannot change our past...we cannot change the fact that people will act in a certain way. We can-not change the inevitable. The only thing we can do is play on the one string we have, and that is our attitude...I am con-vinced that life is 10% what happens to me and 90% how I react to it. And so it is with you...we are in charge of our Attitudes.

—CHARLES SWINDOLL

A key point to remember is that when you begin your anger work-out, the process is ongoing. When you stop doing any of the work-outs, your old counterproductive anger habits are likely to reemerge. The more you do the exercises, the less chance there is to be hurt by your old anger habits. Eventually, you will be able to do the work-out exercises on an automatic basis. This will help you to be more productive in all aspects of your life. You will be a more loving person, better parent, a more effective employee and live longer, because managing your anger helps you to manage your life.

This Anger Work-Out Is Recommended For People

- Who want to control their anger
- Who have trouble with their emotions
- Who want to learn about their emotions
- Who want to take charge of their emotions

Purpose of An Anger Work-Out

This work-out will familiarize you with three essential, components of anger:

- Thoughts
- Bodily responses
- Behavior.

Which of these is hardest for you to monitor or change?

Developing skill in managing these components will help you control your anger, a prerequisite for working your anger program. Work-out #1 is technical, so take your time doing it.

My Daily Log/Work-Out Notes

_____

_____

_____

An important assumption of the anger work-out process is that the full experience of your anger (an emotional state) must include a fusion of <u>thoughts, actions, and bodily reactions</u>. When these components are dissociated, we are left with something other than a true "anger state" e.g., frustration or hurt. Write about your expression of anger now.

_____

_____

_____

_____

_____

Alternatives To An Anger Reaction is to Rethink:

<u>To Change Your Expression of Anger, You Must Change Your Thinking. Change</u> what you say to yourself in your head, in response to the external event.
- Take time to rethink on what has provoked you.
- Use a planned relaxation technique
- Stay calm and keep your cool
- Ask yourself if you are overreacting, justifying your right to be angry, or taking thing too seriously.

Basic Concepts To Understand About Anger Management

To Change Your Expression of Anger, You Must Change Your Thinking. Rethink, Change what you say to yourself in your head, in response to the external event about you.

- Anger is an emotion
- Reason is not employed when we are angry.
- Anger is the result of jumping to conclusions about an outcome.
- Anger creates a sense of energy, excitement and negative aliveness
- Anger is self-serving
- Anger is addictive/obsessive thinking you can't let go.
- Anger is about power and control
- Anger is used to intimidate, instill fear, and as an outlet to get rid of one's inner poison/toxins.
- You do not have a license to hurt or abuse another with your anger.
- No one has given you permission to hurt them because of your inability to handle your life's problems.
- When you are angry, you are out of control, not the other person.
- Others may provoke you to anger, but you do not have to respond angrily. When you respond as others want, they have the power to control you.
- No one is the cause of you responding angrily. You have freedom of choice.
- When you get mad, you are exercising power or seeking to avenge yourself.
- You get some pleasure from hurting others, if you get angry repeatedly.
- If you get angry repeatedly, you are unable to control your feelings of anger.
- Are you in control of your anger or is it controlling you?

Draw a picture of your anger.

Anger is triggered by external events called provocations, which create anger thoughts, anger arousal, and angry actions. All of these stimulate each other until they are fused together, in an anger feedback loop that leads to destructive consequences. An angry outburst can be likened to a hurricane or tornado, as the center of the energy gets smaller, the tension becomes greater, making it harder to generate productive actions to change. And productive actions cannot be made when the anger feedback loop is completely fused. Your anger work out will prevents fusion or confusion.

How Emotional Anger Works
Thoughts—They are thoughts created by you and they correspond to the following pattern.

- **Provocations** → External events that trigger your anger
- **Actions** → Anger actions create→ Arousal →
- **Anger Thoughts** → Anger Arousal → Angry Actions

THINK—BEFORE YOU ACT
Let's Take Action Now
Use this problem solving technique to solve a current problem
.

STATE YOUR PROBLEM

_____

_____

_____

OUTLINE YOUR RESPONSE

_____

_____

_____

_____

LIST YOUR ALTERNATIVES

_____

_____

_____

WRITE OUT AND VISUALIZE THE CONSEQUENCES

Strategy 1

_____

_____

Positive Consequence   **Negative Consequence**

_____

_____

_____

_____

Strategy 2

_____

_____

Positive Consequence   **Negative Consequence**

_____

_____

_____

_____

How To Manage Your Anger

Learning to control your anger helps you:
- Recognize your temperament.
- Validate your temperament
- Learn to delay action on your temper
- Label and verbalize your feelings
- Think about your options
- Empathize with others.

When you develop inner control of a powerful emotion like anger, you become powerful. When you are controlled by your outer environment, you lose the opportunity to have inner control. To become good at any skill, whether it is controlling your physical expression of anger or your tongue, requires continuous practice.

1. What is your definition of anger? Write it out, is it a good feeling or bad feeling?

2. Describe your bodily reactions e.g. tightness of throat:
   a. What part of your body, muscle grouping do you feel the emotion of anger?

3. Are you able to think about your body reactions when you are angry?

4. Are you able to think about what caused you to get/be angry, when you are angry?

5. What do you feel when you are angry?

    a.   Out of control

    b.   Powerful

    c.   Powerless

6.   Write how you feel about anger and your angry feelings.

Ten Steps to Control Your Anger:
1. Make a list of the things that make you mad, and memorize it.
2. Talk about you feelings, let people know when things bother you.
3. When you feel angry, do something with the energy. Slowly breathe in and out ten times. On the exhale, spread you fingers apart widely and imagine the negative energy leaving your body as you do so.
4. When you feel the urge to strike out at someone, raise your shoulders, as you breathe in deeply; rapidly lower your shoulders as you exhale. Notice your jaw muscles, shoulders, hands, chest, and torso muscles. Get in touch with what you are angry about, and with whom you are angry. And think of what situation from your past childhood made you angry.
5. Make peace with yourself and the person who is the object of your anger. Forgive yourself first. Then apologize to the other person for your lack of control.
6. Mentally visualize two paths, (there is an exercise in the book "Light the Fire Within You," that teaches you how to visualize). Have one of these paths be positive, pleasant, and full of light. Have the other path be dark, gloomy, and depressive. Then send your angry feelings down the dark path and over the cliff.
7. Notice if you feel like yelling, screaming, or hitting. Before you act on your anger, think of why you are angry. Is your angry feeling legitimate, or did you create a situation to justify your need to be angry?
8. Talk your way through your anger. Tell yourself you can change from being a reactor of your emotions to being a processor. Notice your thoughts, change negative thoughts to positive.

9. Change the image you have of yourself from "blowing your stack, to being a cool headed person." Whenever you are able to control your anger, reinforce it by saying something kind to yourself.

10. Daily seek ways to change your image, inner thoughts, and outer behavior, so the two match.

Additional Things You Can Do to Control Anger

11. See yourself as a kind person.

12. Seek to become a thinker rather than an emotional reactor. To be an emotional reactor is to be out of control of the self. An emotional reactor discharges and wastes valuable energy needed by the brain to process information When you are an emotional reactor you deplete your body of vital minerals and nutrients (calcium, protein, B complex vitamins, Vitamin C, zinc, manganese, potassium)

Pay attention to your feelings. Remember to validate your feelings by asking yourself these questions—What am I feeling, Why am I feeling this way?, What were the precipitating circumstances to cause me to feel this way, How often do I feel this way, and Who am I emulating?

14. Work through negative emotions as soon as they emerge.

15. Listen to hear what the other person is saying to you. When in doubt, ask for clarification.

16. Listen with the intent to understand. Repeat back to the other person in your words what you think you heard.

17. Notice your body, its space, the body of others and their space.

18. Give others freedom of space and they will honor your space.

In Addition To Learning To Manage Your Anger, It is Better To Practice Self-Control.

The Following Are Suggestions To Help Manage Your Anger:

1. Work on being congruent on both inside and outside yourself.
2. Learn to organize your immediate environment.
3. Put things back as you find them to help create order and stability for yourself.
4. Seek to be the same all the time.
5. Learn to organize your life by keeping a daily "To Do List." Prioritize all your daily activities into A, B, C, D, give A, activities highest priority, B's next etc.
6. Never settle for less than the best effort, best preparation, best outcome, preceded by your best follow through. Be your own coach. Push yourself to be your best, and tell yourself you can do whatever you decide.
7. Do a kind act each day for yourself and someone else.
8. Give yourself permission to be gentle with your and others.
9. Practice ways to be gentle, and kind to yourself and others.
10. Do deep breathing exercises ten minutes, two times a day.
11. Learn to meditate, and practice it for twenty minutes, two times a day. The techniques on how to meditate are listed in the book "Light The Fire Within You," by Dr. Ida Greene. Go through the exercises below to be in better control of your bothersome emotions.

A) How do you feel after expressing these emotions?

    a.   Anger—

    b.   Revenge—

    c.   Jealousy—

    d.   Resentment—

B) Do you feel happy, tired, or sad?

C) Do you like the way you feel? (If your answer is yes, it would be wise to get professional counseling to help you cope with these feelings)

Identify the words you use when interacting with others. For one week, monitor your inner self-talk and outer behavior. Write down your bodily reactions, your breathing, clenched teeth, heavy breathing, tight neck or shoulder muscles, tight jaws, hot ears or other body parts, rigid, tense body posture, balled fist, rolled eyes. Write other bodily reactions you have that I did not list. Record your daily results below.

    1. Day one—

    2. Day two—

    3. Day three—

    4. Day four—

    5. Day five—

6. Day six—

7. Day seven—

If you learn to empower yourself first before you attempt to help another, you will be able to raise your self-esteem and the self-esteem of those around you. Avoid the use of words, or tasks that robs you of energy, drive, and vitality. When you learn how to state and set a goal for yourself for six months, it will enhance your feelings of self-worth.

To change or modify behaviors you now experience, learn to monitor your inner self talk. It affects how you see yourself and others. Soon you will see and experience yourself different and see others differently. Other people mirror back to you what you say, do, and how you behave.

Can you identify and describe what motivates you to face life each day? What motivates you to move forward in life?

List things you can do to be happy or enjoy life more:

-
-
-

Are you in touch with the dark side of yourself? Do you know that the following emotions can lower your self-worth/self-esteem? When did you last have these feelings?

What can you do to minimize or eliminate the emotions below?

Resentment

Envy /Jealousy

Anger

How To Respond When Another Person Is Angry
1. Listen Actively:
   • Make eye contact
   • Move to a neutral area in the conversation
   • Let the person vent
   • Paraphrase what the person says, "Let me make sure I understand you...You are saying you are concerned about..."
2. Do Not Take The Situation Personally
3. Acknowledge Your Feelings And The Other Person's "I can see that you feel strongly about this. Can we discuss this further at...?"
4. Maintain eye contact, and say to the person, "You are shouting. This is inappropriate behavior. Let's discuss this tomorrow at...o'clock..."

How to Handle An Angry Person or Volatile Situation
   • Use A Problem Solving Approach.
   • Identify and state the problem
   • Differentiate between facts, opinions, and feelings
   • Brainstorm alternative solutions
   • Explore the consequences of each solution
   • Select a solution or course of action
   • Evaluate the results

How to Control An Angry Person
   • When the person is exploding, maintain eye contact and listen.
   • Distance yourself at least four arm lengths away from the person.
   • Remain calm—stand or sit still.
   • Assume an "open" posture with your hands up.
   • Speak softly when the other person's voice is raised.
   • Call the person by name
   • Do not touch, point, order, scold, challenge, interrupt, argue, belittle, intimidate, or threaten the angry person.
   • Acknowledge the other person's feelings; express regret

about the problem if appropriate.
- Get permission to ask questions.
- Find out what triggered the event, see if there are under-lying feelings of fear, anxiety, humiliation, or frustration.
- Help the person get control over the situation by asking questions, or offering solutions.

Exercises To Identify Anger
1.   Write your definition of anger, and say if anger is a good or bad feeling.

2.   Describe your bodily reactions when you are angry e.g. tightness of throat:

    a.   What part of your body, muscle groups responds when you are angry?

3.   Are you able to think about your body reactions when you are angry?

4.   Are you able to think about what caused you to get/be angry, when you are angry?

5.   How soon after your expression of anger, can you relax?

6.   What do you feel when you are angry and why?

    a.   Out of control

    b.   Powerful

    c.   Powerless

7.   Conflict is sometimes unavoidable, when you are angry. What is your method to handle conflict?

Anger Work-Out Practice

1.   Choose one behavior from the following list, making sure the one you choose is not something you want to change. (Your goal is to practice watching your self, not to change your behavior.) Next to the behavior you choose, write how you will measure it (frequency or interval).

Feelings of anger

Making telephone calls

Watching television

Self-monitor your self-selected behavior for five days. At the end of each day, transfer your data into a graph grid already prepared.

Days   1   2   3   4   5

_____

Number of times
or average length
of time the → __ __ __ __ __ __ __ __
behavior occurred
NOW TAKE ACTION

After you have practiced self-monitoring, begin to self-monitor the frequency of your anger for seven days (the longer, the
better). Measure your data by moving pennies or toothpicks
from one pocket to another, or use some other way that is con-
venient for you. To make it easier for you, here is your daily
data sheet and graph grid.
Number of times
you got angry

7							
6							
5							
4							
3							
2							
1							
0	1	2	3	4	5	6	7	*days*

We are all artists, creating the experiences of our life. Our thoughts and emotions are the brushes that sweep across the landscape of existence, to create our experiences. The following article was written in the September issue of the Science of Mind magazine. Artist, see the scenes of life from a creative perspective. They are always searching out the play of light against dark, rough against smooth, shades of color and hue, not labeling any of it good or bad, but valuing everything as useful in creating something beautiful and new. We all can take time to look at the world, to take notice of the beauty in rotting wood, cracked cement, bare trees, and department store walls. We can see the rhythms of traffic and the flight of the birds as part of the whole tapestry of our world. What might happen if for one day, we all viewed the world through an artist's eyes to discover how to use everything to create scenes of beauty and greatness? What if we gave up our judgements about what or who is right or wrong and entered into each relationship we encountered during the day as if we had never met before? In the end we would see that we are the artists of our life, just as we are right now." Truly love is the only answer.

Love Is The Only Answer

Love is patient and kind. Love is not jealous or boastful; it is not arrogant or rude. Love does not insist on having its own way; it is not irritable or resentful; it does not rejoice at wrong, but rejoice in the right. No person's life is without obstacles, problems or setbacks. We cannot always avoid obstacles. It is not important to live without problems. It is how we respond to and cope with life's problems, that make the difference. When life give you lemons, can you make lemonade out of it; or do you give up, become hopeless, act helpless, and unable to face life each day.

We can love and accept or resist our problems.

SELF-ASSESSMENT LISTENING EXERCISE

To Help With Anger Management

It is easy to confuse hearing words with active listening. Hearing is picking up sounds. Listening is understanding the intended meaning of the sounds you hear. For each question, select one answer that most closely describes your habit of listening. Write usually, sometime, or seldom next to each statement below.

Usually   Sometime   Seldom

1. I maintain good eye contact with a speaker.
2. I determine the validity of an idea by his or her appearance and delivery.
3. I try to match my thoughts and feelings with whoever is speaking to me.
4. I listen for facts rather than the message.
5. I try to get into the meaning of what is said.
6. I ask questions for clarification to show I care.
7. I withhold judgment of what is being said until a person is through speaking.
8. While others are talking to me, I am thinking of what I will say.

If you chose **Usually** for numbers 1, 3, 5, and 7, or **Seldom** for numbers 2 and 6 you are a good listener.
If you checked **Seldom** more than two times, your listening skill could stand improvement. Write your comments or reflections here.

On Developing Patience

The qualities of patience and understanding are much needed in our world. I contribute to the fulfilling of this need by being patient with myself and others, and I give understanding to all.

My capacity for patience increases as I express an attitude of understanding. I find new understanding and greater insight in my daily giving and living by having a patient attitude.

Patience and understanding contribute to the sharing of my thoughts and ideas with others. And the relationships in my life are blessed because of this.

Being patient and understanding gives me a greater sense of oneness with God. I realize it is the Universal mind of God that is working in and through me to establish love, harmony, and understanding.

In my steadfast and appreciative approach to life I make a valuable contribution to my world, and all people everywhere.

Begin Now

Until one is committed, there is hesitancy, the chance to draw back, always ineffectiveness.

Concerning all acts of initiative, there is one elementary truth—the ignorance of which kills countless ideas and splen - did plans:

That the moment one definitely commits oneself, then prov - idence moves too.

All sorts of things occur to help one that would never oth - erwise have occurred.

A whole stream of events issues from the decision, raising in one's favor, all manner of unforeseen incidents and meetings and material assistance which no man could have dreamed would have come his way.

Whatever you can do, or dream you can, begin it.

Boldness has genius, power and magic in it. Begin it now!
—Goethe

Factors That Lower Our Self-Esteem
- Disrespectful behavior, self-limiting beliefs, or negative thoughts.
- Ridicule/embarrassment, shame, confusion, hurtful words
- Inadequate support system for bonding, ineffective family member/s
- Tendency to be, do, act to gain acceptance or belong
- Praise and punishment, both act as a positive or negative reinforcer and has the ability to influence your behavior.
- To be treated different from others in the family or group.

Can you think of a time when this happened to you? Select the ones above that apply to you.

Write down self-limiting beliefs, thoughts, or behaviors you see in yourself.

A. Where did you hear these statements?

B. Write the name of the person whom you heard say the remark below. Put your name if you made the remark. is boring, no fun, stupid

Say the above statements aloud. "Do you feel energized, or tired?"

Why?

Listed below are some examples of positive beliefs/thoughts, attitudes, and behaviors, note the ones you are likely to say:

a. This is easy—e.g. this is like me, Ida
b. I can do this
c. This is fun
d. I am good at this
e. I am smart
f. Learning something new is exciting and fun

Say the above statements aloud. Do they make you feel <u>good</u> or <u>bad</u>? Why?

Stop what you are doing now and write down three positive beliefs, positive self-enhancing statements, then say them aloud to yourself. E.g.

a. I am intelligent

b. I can figure this out,

c.

d.

e.

Which category of beliefs above has affected your self-esteem, the positive or negative beliefs? Why?

Affirmations For High Self-Esteem
<u>Look in the Mirror Every Morning and Affirm</u>:

1. I nurse my inner child with love in my heart, and I am healed of past errors.
2. I now support my inner child. I am healed of any sense of low self-worth. I am worthy and deserving of all the good I can imagine and then some.
3. It is O.K. for the little child in me to succeed, be successful, have wealth and enjoy life.
4. I approve of my inner child, s/he is O.K.
5. I am a spiritual being living a spiritual life. There is no place doubt, anxiety, or fear.
6. I know that what I experience is a result of my thinking, so I eliminate all negativity from my mind. I accept my good.
7. I now know the truth, I live in a spiritual universe. I see myself as a spiritual being, and I have dominion over my life.
8. I have a power within me that maintain and sustain me, my Father/Mother God and I are one.
9. I am blessed with an abundance of all the good life has to offer; this includes money, and money substance.
10. I am free of all lack, self-limiting thoughts and beliefs.
11. I have perfect health, vision, and hearing. I am total perfection.
12. My way in life is made clear, I listen and follow my intuition. I now call forth Divine Order and clarity.
13. I am filled with enthusiasm, life, love and joy. I like life and living.
14. I am free of all confusion and congestion. I have perfect circulation in all my affairs.

A PRAYER TREATMENT FOR YOUR RIGHT RELATIONSHIP

I Accept The Right Love In My Life.

As I speak my word for right companionship and love,
*   I reaffirm my faith in divine guidance.*

I acknowledge and accept the life, and light of God's per -
*   fect creation.*

I accept the spirit within me, which is already one with the
*   one whose love I am to share.*

This spirit is attracting the two of us now, and we will meet
*   when the time is exactly right.*

If we have already met, or if the one I am with now is in
*   truth the right one for me, then I shall know it, and I*
*   will receive unmistakable guidance from my high inner*
*   Self.*

I am at peace, as I release this treatment into the universe.

I know that it is done.

And all is well with my soul.

*   —ANON*

I ACCEPT MY SELF, HEALTH, AND WEALTH

It is right, and just for me to have my needs met.

It is right and just for me to ask for and receive what I
*   want.*

It is right and acceptable by me for others to love and
*   show their appreciation to me.*

I am deserving of love, affection, right treatment, respect,
*   and honors from others.*

I am created in the image and likeness of God, it feels
*   good.*

I am created in the image of God, who is perfection of
*   body, mind, and soul.*

God cares for me and She provides for all my needs.

I do not need to ask, because my loving mother, God knows
*   what I need.*

I am proud to have rich, royal, wise and spiritual lineage.

All of my needs are abundantly supplied; I now cease all
*   worry and concern so that God can perform.*

I accept that I am loved beyond measure by a God who wants only the best for me.
I give up all struggle and allow God to point the way.
I am patient with myself and God as I evolve to my highest spiritual self.
I am becoming a better human being each day; worthy to be called a child of God.
I accept all of God's creation, starting with myself.

20 Laws Of Self Esteem

1. Accept yourself confidently as you are.
2. Never do anything in private that you would not want the world to know.
3. Think the best and expect the best of yourself at all times.
4. Become your own best friend.
5. Perform to the best of your ability in all your endeavors.
6. Put no other person before yourself; including your friend, child, mother, father, lover, husband, or wife.
7. Develop and nourish your inner self continuously.
8. Listen and be open to your inner prompting and follow your intuition.
9. Hold yourself in high esteem and accept that there is a larger force in the universe that operates independent of you.
10. Know that there is a force that keeps the universe together, and that all things are always working out as they should.
11. Think for yourself, trust your judgement, and make your own decisions.
12. Worry less and trust your decision-making ability.
13. Become a decision-maker.
14. Be a mover and doer of goodwill for yourself and all of humanity.
15. Treat yourself with kindness, dignity and self-respect.

16. Guard the words that fall from your lips. Make them words of joy, happiness, and goodwill towards all, including yourself.
17. Avoid comparing yourself to others.
18. Expect the best from all people at all times including yourself.
19. Constantly seek ways to improve yourself.
20. Strive towards excellence in all you do, say, and think.

Light The Fire Within You

Exercises to Empower Yourself and Increase Feelings of Self-Worth

1. Write <u>words</u> you feel <u>best describe you</u>.

2. What <u>words</u> would others use to describe you? <u>Why</u>?

3. Are you <u>excited daily</u> about <u>getting up for work</u>? Why?

4. Why were you created?

To do <u>what</u>?

Where?

When?

For whom?

5. What kind of work would you like to do to express your Higher Self?

6. If you could live any place in the U.S. or the world, where would it be?

7. If you could do what you wanted, what would you be? What would you have?

What would you do?

8. What do you think successful people do to become successful?

9. How much education do you want?

Do you feel this will occur?

10. Will you go to college?

Will you graduate from college?

11　What is your favorite food?

Car?

12　What is your idea of fun?

Self-Esteem, Are You Ready To Change?
Primary Factors That Shape Our Self-Esteem:

1. As you go through this list, place a (+) or (-) by any category that evokes a positive or negative reaction in you and state why, underneath each section.

    A　.Parental readiness and acceptance

    B.　Sex of child

    C.　Cultural concept of beauty, what it means to be Beautiful.

    D.　Physical and emotional health of mother

    E.　Physical health of infant

    F.   Cultural customs, folklore, beliefs, ethnic identity and pride

    G.   Behavior expectation—what you needs to do, say to be a member of the clan.

    H.   What is your support system for bonding (grand-parent, aunt, uncle). Do you have a substitute for an ineffective family member/s?

    I.   How do you feel about your extended family members?

2.   Can you identify beliefs you hold, that block your personal, professional, social, or spiritual growth?

3.   What can you do today to change the following, your:
    a.   Beliefs —

    b.   Attitude —

    c.   Self-Respect—

    d.   Self-Acceptance—

4. Self-Confidence—Write your definition of self-confidence

5. List the factors that affect your self-confidence:

-

-

-

-

To Light The Fire Within You™, Learn how to be in control of negative emotions and destructive urges. List what you will do about:

a. Resentment —

b. Envy —

c. Jealousy —

d. Anger/Hostility —

e. Rage —

f. Fears —

PURPOSE, A REASON FOR LIVING

*Purpose gives meaning to life. It gives Joy, and
    Zest to living.*

What is your Desire, your Dream?

*When our eye is on our goal, we are not so easily
    disturbed by things around us.*

*Purpose awakens new trains of thoughts in our mind.
    Our purpose directs these trains of thought into new
    fields of achievement.*

*To succeed in life we must have some great purpose in
    mind; some goal toward which we would like to
    achieve. Find a purpose, today!*

                            —ANON

MY SELF-ESTEEM

Using a scale of 0 through 10 (0 lowest, 5 average, 10 highest) choose the number that indicates how you feel at this moment and the number that indicates how you want to feel in each of the following areas of self-esteem.

SELF-ESTEEM AREAS	I FEEL	I WANT TO FEEL
Sense of UNIQUENESS (Special+)		
Sense of Belonging		
Sense of Power		
Sense of Joy		
Sense of Wonder		
Sense of Integrity		
Sense of Mastery		
Sense of Purpose		

These are the areas of my self-esteem I choose to develop:

_____

_____

_____

Chapter 5

Communicate Effectively To Be Understood

Effective communication is a combination of inner and interpersonal communication. Factors that impact the way we communicate are the eye, ear, mouth, jaw, teeth, vocal cords, lungs, and diaphragm. Communication is a simple yet complex process. Often the message we send to an individual is received differently, than we intended and has a connotation other than that sent. Ask yourself what can you do to send a powerful message that has clarity and impact? You can start by developing more effective listening skills.

The three channels through which we process information are Visual, Auditory and Kinesthetic. The characteristic behavior of each modality, is individual and group communication.

The three forms of communication are: Monologue, one way communication; Dialogue, inner communication two way communication; Interpersonal communication; Outer Dialogue, communication between three or more persons.

The communication process uses three types of communication vehicle. They are verbal, nonverbal, and creative expression. The transmission channel to impart a message is the written word, spoken word, and the expressive word (drama, music, Sign Language). When you communicate with others, using the spoken word the basic Communication Process will consist of a sender, the message, and a receiver to decode the message to get feedback from the receiver. There are three factors that impact the way we communicate, they are unresolved conflict, environment (positive negative), and suppressed negative emotions like anger. The anatomical parts of the body involved in communication are the eye, ear, mouth/jaw/teeth, vocal cord, lungs, and diaphragm.

Learn to communicate so that others get the message you

intended to send rather a confused message, double, or no message. You do this by stating your message clearly, succinctly, with feeling. When people get your message, they act upon what you say. They *react* to what you say. When there is hostility, or anger, in your tone of voice, or if you send a confused/double message, it will be detected and you will get a response to verify what you sent.

How We Express What We Hear

The way we communicate, the words we use, the gestures we employ, our tone of voice, our mannerisms, and idiosyncrasies all make a statement about, who we are, and sends a visual message to others about us. This can be to our advantage or disadvantage. Naturally you would prefer it to be to your advantage. Therefore you should communicate in a way that others get the message you intend to send rather than a confused message, or double message.

When we talk, we communicate information through our words (word usage) ideological orientation, voice inflection (tone/pitch/volume/timbre), gestures in our expression of feeling with our head, hands, arms, shoulders, and all body language (posture).

Communicating to get your message across is essential to success in all aspects of your daily life. Each of us uses words to express our thoughts and feelings through one or more representational systems. The traditional ways are through a Visual, Kinesthetic, or Auditory Channel. Do you know which system you predominantly use? Do you speak one way and behave in another way? If so you are sending the other person a double or confusing message. The result you get may have been interpreted as emotional or verbal (mental) abuse.

How To Get The Best From Others

Strategies you can employ to facilitate better communication include problem solving techniques and decision-making skills. If you desire to give feedback that support others, be honest and show compassionate in your feedback, use language that builds and support, and think before you speak. Your timing, and intention to be fair, should be foremost in mind. Always let your communication show caring, empathy, and concern.

Communication is more than the use of words, thrown at people in a random, disorganized fashion. Effective communication is the use of select words in an organized, deliberate order that is designed to elicit a positive response or behavior from an individual so they get your message and respond positively. Learn to become aware of the differences in your communication patterns, and make them work to your advantage.

Give feedback that supports. Let your feedback to others be honest and use language that builds and supports. Think before you speak. Your timing, intention, and unconscious omission or commissions can hinder or hurt the effectiveness of what you are trying to communicate.

Remember, to communicate more effectively:

1. Specify what you want to happen.
2. Request small changes in behavior from others.
3. Start by making small changes in your behavior.
4. Specify what behavior you are willing to change to get an Agreement.
5. Be Cooperative—show others you want to compromise.
6. Be Tolerant of yours and others imperfections.
7. Express your feelings, but express them calmly.
8. To incorporate caring in your voice when speaking, watch your:
    a. Voice tone
    b. Voice pitch—start with a soft whisper and gradually increase your tone of voice.
9. Be a Friend—Act Friendly!
10. Be Pleasant—Develop a positive attitude

How To Get The Best From Yourself

The way we communicate, the words we use, the gestures we employ, the tone of voice we use, our mannerisms and idiosyncrasies, all make a statement about who we are and sends a message to others about us. This can be to our advantage or disadvantage. Naturally, you prefer it to be to your advantage. State your messages in a clear, succinct manner, with feeling so people "act positively upon what you say," rather than "react negatively to what you say."

Learn how to communicate to make yourself understood, know how to detect when there is a break down in communication, and be able to identify how it occurred and what you can do to correct the break down in communication.

Communication blockers are your attitude, past experiences, the individual interpretation of feelings, and your emotions — past and present. The factors that cause ineffective communication are stress and negative emotions such as anger, envy, fear, hate, jealousy, revenge, malice, self doubt, jealousy, greed, unresolved conflict, confusion, fixed beliefs (closed mind), assumed understanding, negative attitude or outlook.

Identify and describe the action you desire, and ignore the motive of others. Be in control of your fear, anxiety, and pay attention to your breathing. Excessive or erratic jaw/mouth movement can cause you to swallow your word. Take time now to critique practice the above-mentioned exercises. Write your observations and experiences below. Breathing is shallow, fears and anxiety level is high, My mouth movement is relaxed/stiff, I swallow my word, I do not enunciate clearly.

1.

2.

The art of communication can be likened to a well orchestrated, symphony, a majestic sunset, or a finely tuned watch; all are in perfect harmony. To get the most from your communication with others, pay as much attention to their unspoken behavior (non-verbal communication) as you do to the words they speak. This is especially true for children, the physically ill, the elderly, and persons whose culture is different from your own. Effective communication is a sacred relationship. It is an art form.

TREATMENT FOR RIGHT RELATIONSHIP
I want to really bless the people I deal with, I want
to feel good about all my relationships.
Therefore I now speak my word for complete peace of mind
in all my relationships. The God in me is one with the
God in all people. I believe this wholeheartedly and I
accept it. So I relate in a healthy manner to everyone I
encounter today.
If this includes someone who usually irritates me,
I will refuse to let that happen.
I will be in control of my emotions rather the other person.
I affirm right now that God's love through me is already
blessing the person I have in mind. I am free and so
are they.
—ANON

ACCEPT THE POWER OF YOUR HEALING WORD
Because I believe in God's power to heal. As I read words
of healing, I accept the truth of what they say,
and I become receptive to the power there.
I now speak my own word, to accept the right
solution to my problem.
I believe God is Love, and I accept that Love.
I believe God is Life and that every cell of my body
responds
to the healing power of that life as my life now.
I am grateful for these truths, and I accept them.
—ANON

Slay The Dragon Inside
To Light The Fire Within You

An understanding of *ethics* can help us tame the unrefined parts of our character so that we participate more fully as member of the human race. All of us need a set of principles or guidelines to follow that will help us make just and fair decisions in our professional and personal interactions. A code of ethics gives us a standard for behaving based on the principles we value as important in our personal and professional relations.

Some of the principles that are universally agreed upon as being just and fair for all people are: Fairness, (keen sense of right and wrong), Integrity (set of rules to live by that one's behavior match one's word), Respect (for oneself and others), no Stealing/Cheating (respecting the property/rights of others), Human Dignity (courtesy, acknowledgment), Trust (dependable, consistent), Honesty (to tell the truth regardless of the consequences to oneself), Quality or Excellence, Desire to help your fellow man, or be of service, Patience or Tolerance with the weak or lame, Nurturance or concern about another's welfare, and Support or Encouragement.

Ethics is a standard of conduct that governs your behavior, interactions and relationships with others. It tells how you treat other people. Most of us have an internal set of rules by which to live, that tells us which things are acceptable and which are not. Although, for each of us, there may be individual differences about what is ethical or not ethical. This is why you may feel another person has a distorted, or misdirected perception of proper protocol they employ in a given situation. What is happening is that the two of you have a different set of values (ethics) by which you govern your life and affairs. When this happens, there will be a communication breakdown or a difference of opinion as to what each of you considers to be right or wrong, acceptable or non-acceptable.

Our code of ethics may come from the following sources or a combination of these: generational or parental values of one's ancestors, family tradition of acceptable/approved behavior for the family, Holy Bible (Golden Rules e.g. Do unto others as you would have them do unto you), books (Bhagavad-Gita, Koran, Tao), literature, philosophy courses, history books, movies (The Greatest Story Ever Told). What set of rules do you have that dictates how you treat others? Write your answer below.

Who taught you what values were important and why?

Did you learn these values in the home, church, or school?

Do you remember how old you were when you first heard these do's and don'ts?

Write out your ethical values or set of rules by which you live.

RIVERS...
Rivers hardly ever run in a straight line.
Rivers are willing to take ten thousand meanders
And enjoy every one.
And grow from everyone
When they leave a meander
They are always more
Than when they entered it.

When rivers meet an obstacle,
They do not try to run over it;
They merely go around it

But they always get to the other side.

Rivers accept things as they are,
Conform to the shape they find the world in
Yet nothing changes things more than rivers;
Rivers move even mountains into the sea.

Rivers hardly ever are in a hurry ——
Yet is there anything more likely
To reach the point it sets out for
Than a river?
                              —JAMES DILLET FREEMAN

Chapter 6

Say Goodbye To Your Smallness
Say Hello To Your Greatness

You are greater than you think. You are part of the great I AM of the universe and that makes you special. The great I AM presence is everywhere, all encompassing, in everyone, at the same time. This I AM presence is abundant, unlimited, it is perfection, wholeness, health, wealth, and prosperity. You can have as much of this life force as you can accept. It is always available to everyone regardless of their, occupation, profession, education, or status in life, whether you have failed at something, or exceeded greatly. It asks only two things of you; that you be of service to humanity sharing your gift/talent and that you be the best that you can be all the time. You may ask, if the great I AM presence has all of these attributes (perfection, health, wealth, love, joy, peace, harmony and right relationships) and you and I are part of it, why doesn't our lives work better?

It is because we have separated ourselves from this life force. Everything is consciousness, meaning it is a state of mind. If our mind was open to accept and believe that we were Great; that, we came from Greatness, we would act differently. To be Great, we must <u>Think Great thoughts</u>, <u>Act in a Great way</u> and <u>Be Great each moment of the day.</u>

Greatness is acceptance of your intrinsic worth to make a difference in the universe. When you undervalue who you are, the world will undervalue who you are. The only limiting thoughts are those you impose upon yourself. Humility is not the same as smallness or weakness. You can be both great and humble at the same time. Humility allows you to be great without arrogance. The only person who can block your greatness is you, because you are in control of your thoughts

What are the mental blocks to your Greatness that keeps you

locked into mediocrity? Most of us unknowingly say and do things that bring out the worst in us rather than the best. *We sab - otage our Greatness by acting and thinking small.* In the word of Nelson Mandela, he says, "the planet is not served by you playing and acting small." There are five major blocks that enslaves us to Smallness and prevents us from embracing our Greatness.
They are:

- Limited thinking (Thinking Small)
- Negative thinking → Negative Attitude
- Misinterpretation of spiritual principles
- Fear of money (poverty mind set/poor me)
- Fear of success.

To be a success in life we have to honor the Greatness within ourselves and those around us. If you cannot see the greatness in others, you will never see it in yourself.

There are many Masters among us, do you see or recognize them? If you cannot see mastery in others, it may be that your mind is filled with envy, jealousy, strife, anger, resentment, hate or hostility toward persons who are trying to be better and do better. What are you thinking on most of your waking hours? Do you continually think positive thoughts about yourself and others or do you allow your mind to be filled with negative thoughts? Do you think the worst outcome most of the time? If so you will need to take control of your body, mind, and soul (spirit). The essence of you is abundance, prosperity, joy, peace, harmony, love, and positive relationships. Will you choose Greatness or will you continue to think, act, and live from your Smallness? The choice is yours, what do you choose to think, thoughts of Greatness or Smallness? The invisible you accept becomes manifest in your outer world.

Do you know the mental blocks to your Greatness? For things to change in your life, you will need to change the way you think, act and react. You will need to unlearn some things and learn new thought patterns or beliefs. You are learning on a continuous basis. All learning takes place on a subliminal level. Therefore you are learning when you listen to the negative conversation of others, and you do nothing to erase or block this information from entering into the computer of your mind. Remember garbage in, means garbage out, or smallness or limited thinking in, smallness or limited thinking out. Do you surround yourself with limited thinking persons or do you surround yourself with masterful, positive, possibility thinking people? *We become, like the people with whom we associate on a con - tinuous basis.* Who are you aspiring to become, your bigger and best self, or your limited, small self?

In addition to the five major mental blocks, There are five minor mental blocks that will prevent you from experiencing your Greatness. They are:

- Laziness due to apathy or inertia
- Doubt, Uncertainty, or Fear
- Negative Self-Concept/identity and low Self-Image (have just enough to survive or pay your bills. What about a surplus with plenty to spare and share?
- Faulty Beliefs (it is better to give than receive) It is OK for both.
- Envy or Resentment for people who are wealthy or have money

How To Move Through Your Blocks

1. Use mind mapping, write or draw what you want to have. Use different felt colored pencils to activate the right side of the brain.
2. Write the essence of your goal as an affirmation.
3. Repeat the affirmation ten times, three times a day with playful body movements.
4. Recite the affirmation while listening to Classical music. Classical music stimulates the reticular activating center in the right lobe of the brain, where creativity takes place.

5. Reinforce the new belief with visual stimuli. Place the affirmation in key places in your home where you frequent, bathroom, refrigerator etc.

Other ways, we sabotage our Greatness is to become attached to old hurts and pain from our past. When we replay in our mind, the times someone hurt our feelings or wronged us, it is easy to become mesmerized to feel sorry for ourselves. Then we develop, a "poor me" script and begin to act like a victim. There are no victims in life. We are all willing participants in the pain, hurt, chaos, and drama we create in our lives.

I see life as a stage, from which I can practice and experiment to make life work better for me and have fun in the process. I have watched the drama of my life, some of it is sad, but most of it is bold, exciting, and stimulating. I like excitement, so when things get too boring I look for ways to get me out of my mediocrity. Mediocrity is just another word for Smallness. When I act small or confused, often, I am perceived by others as powerless. When I allow this to happen, I will usually get alone with myself and meditate to find ways I can self correct or change my pattern. It is not easy to break entrenched patterns of which we have received positive or negative reinforcement in the past. It is easy to become attached to the negative emotions of jealousy, envy, strife, hate, revenge, resentment, loss, grief, old hurts, rejection, disappointment, abandonment, or lack and limitation, all keeps us locked into Smallness.

Is your self-concept great or small?

Self-Concept/Self-Identity Assessment

1. Self-Concept (Identity/ Is it: nice person, poor me, be perfect, superiority-inferiority complex, klutz,) what mask/masks do you wear? How do you see yourself? List below:

2. Use your non-dominant hand and write about your self-concept.

3. Use your non-dominant hand, draw a picture of your self-concept.

4. Write one word that describes your self-concept.

5. What self-concept would you write if you were unhampered, or felt unlimited?

• Draw a picture of this person.

• What/Who is the most important thing in your life?

• What is your ultimate purpose in life?

• What do you consider most urgent right now?

• What has produced the most happiness in your life?

• What do you consider your greatest obstacle to success/happiness?

I LOVE MYSELF THE WAY I AM

I love myself the way I am; there is nothing I need to
*   change.*
I'll always be the perfect me; there is nothing to rearrange.
I'm beautiful and capable of being the best me I can and
I love myself just the way I am.
I love you just the way you are; there's nothing you need
*   to do,*
When I feel the love inside myself, it's easy to love you.
Behind your fears, your rage and tears, I see your shining
*   star; and I love you just the way your are.*
I love all people the way they are 'cause I can clearly see
*   that all the things I judge are done by people just like me.*
So, till the birth of peace on earth that only love can bring,
*   I'll help it grow by loving everyone.*
I love myself the way I am, and still I want to grow.
But change outside can only come when deep inside I know
*   I'm beautiful and capable of being the best me I can; and*
*   I love myself, just the way I am,*
I love myself, just the way I am.

—ANON

10 Steps To Learn Self Discipline

1. Notice when you are too hyperactive and unable to focus your thoughts (attention) or energy (nervous, fidgeted).
2. When you are too hyperactive to think, or be calm, take deep breaths, breathe deeply for three minutes or count to ten, three times.
3. Learn to organize your immediate environment by keeping things in order. Put things back as you find them, to help create order and stability for yourself.
4. Work to be a thinker, rather than an emotional reactor.
   A. To be an emotional reactor, is to be out of control of oneself.
   B. An emotional reactor, wastes discharges and wastes valuable energy needed by the brain to process information.
   C. Being an emotional reactor depletes your body of the following minerals and nutrients: calcium, protein, carbohydrate, B complex vitamins, vitamin C, zinc, manganese, and potassium.
5. When you need to make a decision, give yourself two alternative choices before deciding.
6. Pay attention to your feelings. Remember to validate them by asking yourself the following key questions:

   A. What am I feeling?

   B. Why am I feeling this way?

   C. What are the precipitating circumstances causing me to feel this way?

D. How often do I feel this way?

E. Who am I emulating? Mom, dad, grandmother, grandfather, aunt, uncle?

7. Listen more intently to what the other person is saying to you, and ask for clarification if you are unsure. Also do the following:

    A. Listen with the intent to understand.
    B. Repeat back to the other person in your own words what you think you heard.
    C. As a double check for listening, state "I am asking for clarification to be sure I heard you correctly, did you say_____?"

8. Notice your body, its space, and the body of the other person and their space. Give others freedom of space and they will in turn honor your space.

9. Learn to organize your life by keeping a daily "To Do" list to prioritize your activities. Separate them into:

    A.—most important
    B.—next in importance
    C.—least importance

10. Never settle for less than your best effort, best prepa- ration, best outcome, preceded by your follow through. Remember to:

    A. Be your own coach
    B. Push yourself to be your best self

C. Tell yourself you can do what you desire to accomplish because you are the best, you are worthy, and deserving of the best life has to offer.

I Am Worth It

I may sometime cause confusion when I am unclear in my communication, unsure of myself, or uncertain about an outcome, yet I am worth the bother.

I may act timid and fearful sometimes, but please remem - ber I am trying to sort things out in my mind, and I am worth the bother.

Even though you may struggle to understand me, I am worth it.

My friend, I am the other half of you.

I am incomplete without you, and you are incomplete without me.

In some strange way, though we differ in racial composi - tion, thoughts, ideas, and behavior, we are wedded to each other.

I will release you for now, to soar above the heavens. Just remember, whatever disappointment or challenge I face, I deserve the best, for I am worth it.

—Ida Greene

Chapter 7

How To Step Into Your Greatness

To tap into your Greatness, accept that everyone is a unique individual. No one is duplicated throughout the universe, so there is no one with whom to compare. What is your passion? Your passion will lead you to your true purpose in life. What are you so passionate about that you would do even if you did not receive money?

To be great we have to change our life script. This may be a challenge without outside help. It is sometimes difficult for us to see the way we dance through life. This is why I want to live to be 120 years; maybe by then I will have self corrected enough to get a perfect score of 10 in the game of life. Life truly is a game. Sometimes I feel like a winner and other times I feel like a loser. Either way it is my and your life and we can always self correct our path when the emotional pain we endure becomes unbearable. This means that we can change the way we are doing something and in the change process we also change the way we see ourselves thereby creating a new self-image.

The key to personal empowerment is right view, right action, right focus, right effort or activity, right thoughts, and right relationship, which when blended together will provide our right work or livelihood.

It is easy to focus on what is not working in our life; problems are only solutions to be solved so that we rise to our Greatest moment in life. Learn to go with the flow. Let yourself be an open vessel. Get out of the need to control things. Control creates stress and tension; both block our creativity and Divine purpose in life. Learn to let in the sunshine, let in the joy, love, prosperity, abundance, peace, and Greatness. Dance in life like the leaves on a tree, or a blade of grass in the meadows.

113

Step onto the stage of life and say—Yes I will Go, Do, and Be. Take a risk, Be Bold, Be Outrageous, Be Magnificent, Be Royal, Be Gentle With Yourself, Just Be.

JUST BE

The past as glorious as it was can be better.
So let go the tears, old regrets and fears.
Let go, the should, ought to, could have, wish
* I could have, for it truly is in the past.*
Let go the emotional pain, the sadness, the loneliness,
* the lack of acknowledgment.*
Today is a new day. It speaks to you of a new dawning.
Today is a new day of hope, possibilities, and potential.
Grab hold, of that wish, that desire, that dream, regardless
* of how small it seems. Tuck it deep within your bosom.*
Let your imagination soar. Let your spirit soar.
Life is endless. You are eternal.
Move through the negativity, the stagnation, and blockage.
It is time to move. It is time to breathe. It is time to smile.
It is time to laugh.
It is time to live. It is time to be.
Be the miracle you were destined to be.
You are good enough. Be whoever you are.
Be Prosperous, Be magnificent, Be Love, Be Joy,
Just Be, Be .Be.

—IDA GREENE

Life is too much fun to be taken seriously. You are human, you are Divine, you are a miracle, you are a precious gift to the universe. Think Greatness. You are you and that is enough. Be fully present in each moment and enjoy your creations. Keep loving—Love God or your Higher Power, love yourself, and all creation on the planet. We are all part of God's greatest enjoyment. He created you in His image, how can you be nothing less than Great. Accept your Greatness, you are one of God's chosen flowers. You add a special fragrance to life. Breathe deeply and be yourself. Just Be, Be It,

Do It.

114

Do It!

Do It! Today is the day, Don't delay.
Do It! This hour is precious, Use it.
Do It! This thought is valuable, Hold it.
Do It! Keep your vision focused up, Keep it.
Do It! This moment is divine, Cherish it.
Do It! The future is now, Embrace it.
Do It! Someday is today, Go for it.
Do It! Greatness is your right, Own it.
Do It! You are Divine, Accept it.
Do It! No one is standing in your way, Move.
Do It! No one will stop you, Go.
Do It! Life is waiting for you to act, Get started.
Do It! This is the life you have been dying to have, Live It
Do It! Wealth is your birthright, Claim it.
Do It! Action cures fear, Act now.
Do It! Love is the answer to any problem, Try it.
Do It! God wants to help you, Let go and accept help.
Do It! You are lovely, Be it.
Do It! You are special, Believe it.

—IDA GREENE

Affirm Now And Say Aloud To Yourself—
> **I now let go old ways of thinking to make room
> for the new me.**
> **I now accept right action in all I do, right intention,
> right love and my right livelihood. I am a miracle**

The Essence Of You Is—
Perfection, Abundance, Wholeness, Health, Joy, Love, Power, Strength, Knowledge, Wisdom, Peace, Influence, Affluence, and Loving, Positive Relationships. You are a Divine Royal being, who deserves the best life has to offer.

My intuition is always accurate. I am clear minded and focused at making the right decisions. I can always trust and follow my gut instincts. I am aligned with my highest intuitive wisdom. My intuition is always accurate, specific and to the point! It's easy for me to understand what my heart is telling me. I can hear and communicate these deep messages I receive from the Universe. I have an intimate connection to a source of higher intelligence and knowing. I am always listening to my higher self and following it! I am committed to being open and receptive to my intuition.

I now have only generous authentic loving relationships. I am now surrounded by positive loving relationships. I have authentic communication and deep spiritual connections with every being I meet. My relationships are always beautiful and divinely perfect. My mate and I are growing more loving, intimate and trusting with each other every day. Everyone around me is generous, loving and honest with me. They always share with their friends and family fantastic things about me. Even people I don't know are saying good things about me. People rant and rave about how inspiring I am to them. Everyone loves me. Everywhere I go people smile at me and give me a warm vibe.

I have an amazingly powerful relationship with myself. I am always relaxed and confident about my life. I can feel good about loving and accepting myself as I am. I support desires to be, do and have everything I want. The Universe is a safe and sacred place for me to live in. I can feel safe to love all parts of myself that need attention. I am committed to having an amazingly powerful relationship with myself.

I am a secure and confident person. I express myself as a confident and secure person. I communicate easily with everyone about how I live my life with zest, energy and enthusiasm. I am real with everyone. I am a happy person just as I am. I am a very energetic, powerful and enthusiastic being of love. I am committed to being a secure and confident person.

I feel spiritually connected with each person I talk to. I communicate naturally from my heart-space at all times with all beings. I am about being powerful, all-loving and giving gentle warm wisdom to all beings on Earth. I see the Divine within everyone and I easily communicate this to them. I am confident and comfortable looking directly into any human beings eyes. I can now approach any person I meet with a genuine smile, open heart and a positive mental attitude. I am protected at all times because I am an infinite loving source to all people. I am committed to feeling spiritually connected with each person to whom I talk.

My body and mind are radiating with perfect fitness and health. I am experiencing a higher level of physical, mental, emotional strength, spiritual strength and vitality every day. I am committed to work out and I easily do each exercise. I am happy about my life and my body shows it. I now exercise in a healthy, loving and meditative way. I am committed to living in a mind and body that are radiating with perfect fitness and health.

I speak from my heart in challenging situations. I awake each morning trusting that it is safe to be in my heart all day long. I can live my from my heart and it is safe to love from my heart. My heart is continuously expanding and deepening with feelings of peace and love. I now feel a divine love radiating from my whole body, out to everyone on earth. I am committed to speak from my heart during challenging situations.

I sleep deeply and rest completely every night. I awaken each morning feeling refreshed, full of energy and enthusiasm for the day.

I will **only** do inspired actions in my life (meaning doing only what inspires me!)

I will stop, breathe and be with my inner blocks and negativity when they arise, meeting them with a gentle, compassionate, and conscious curious energy.

There are basically two movements of consciousness: Love and Fear. Love is allowing what is and fear is resisting it.
—NIRMALA

I don't know the key to success, but the key to failure is trying to please everybody.
—BILL COSBY

Claim each quality by speaking aloud your special name I AM, before it. For example, I am strong.

I AM
Strong, Wise, Enthusiastic, Successful, Confident, Healthy, Loving, Prosperous,
Happy and a Joy Bringer!
—JOYCE KRAMER

I celebrate myself.
—WALT WHITMAN

I bring Pleasure, Happiness, Cheerfulness and Joy into the lives of others.
—JOYCE KRAMER

AFFIRM DAILY

You have the capacity to believe what you want to believe, so you can build into your mind and heart a belief in the validity of words. Start by thinking upon the ideas expressed through the words. What you think upon grows and expands. Read the above words aloud. Spoken words activate energy that goes to work to bring what you speak into being.

Re-write your reality. At the end of the day, write in your 're-write' journal. Write down your day as if it has g one exactly as you'd like. This can be a lot of fun, and really get into your feelings as you look back over how perfectly your day went.

When you apply these techniques through the heart, this is so very powerful. It moves you forward so rapidly. The more you enjoy it, the more fun you have the more it works.

118

One of the easiest ways to expand your energy and become attractive is through gratitude. Be grateful for what you have right now, and for the vision of what you've created (your desires) and feel that feeling in your heart.

Draw a picture of yourself, or use a photo, and draw money all around you, have your arms opened up and full of money. See yourself as magnet to money; see it coming from all around you. You can see you are open to it, you have the money all around you and it's in your arms and it's coming from everywhere. Do this now.

Remember, no matter what is going on in your life right now, you are so much more than what you are experiencing right now. Focus on your power, focus on who you truly are, focus on your vision of joy.

If you will just get up in the morning and open up your arms and look outside at the beautiful world and say "I am open to life, and I am open to wealth and I am open to a tremendous amount of money and I am open to millions of dollars right now!" Say these words every morning. Open up your arms to life and open up your heart.

LIFE IS A MYSTERY
Life Is a Mystery to be Lived, Not a Problem to be Solved.
—OSHO

There are three basic responses to life. The first is resisting what is. Our body contracts, tightens in and constricts when we feel threatened, out of control or hurt in some way. The second is allowing what is. This is an experience of trust, release and expansion. We interpret life as a safe, loving, nourishing, place, when we relax and let go. Then our lives feel open and spacious. The third response, contains components of the first two, it is a neutral response. When we are detached, we have no opinion; we are free from all forms of judgment and limiting experiences that may arise.

Take a moment to go within, what comes to your mind about how you see yourself. Who comes to mind when you think on those words.

Power

Prestige

Authority

Self-Esteem

Self-Image

Self

Negative Self-Identity

Positive Self-Identity

Instead of thinking that the world is out to get you…think again. Remind yourself that the world is weighted in your favor. This one platform of thought will change your life. When you change how you gear for life, your life is changed. Start thinking this one thought. "The world is weighted in my favor." Isn't this different from what you have been thinking? Start thinking:

> *"The world wants me. The world greets me. The whole world looks to endow me. The crowds of the world lift me high on their shoulders and cheer me so that my travel is hastened and lightened. The whole universe propels me forward. The universe swirls me in joy. I am lifted high. I see over the crowds. I see wonder rushing on its way to me. The scales tip in my favor. The world is weighted in my favor."*

This one switch in your thinking will allow miracles to reach your awareness and tap into your God self, I call the Greatness within. This switch in your thinking is a way to tap into miracles. You have been wary of trouble. Start today to engage in miracle-watching.

Knowing your place in the scale of the universe predicates the goodness that is to come. Your new thinking clears a path for you. It sweeps the old thinking away. One change in the configuration of your thoughts, and everything is changed. You rise to the forefront of your life.

You are a champion of the world. You are a heralder of wonder to come. You are a miracle-watcher. Angels light the way before you. Your new thinking urges them forward. Like a fleet of reindeer, angels leap you forward. They leap to your thoughts. Step into Your Greatness

Use the steps below as a tool to train your mind to see beyond reality

Say aloud:

I accept and honor my Magnificence, it is a body weight of ... ...lbs.

Recognition: There is one Truth in the Universe. It is perfect, whole and complete. Order and organization are everywhere manifest in nature.

Unification: I am one with this Truth. I am aligned and unified with the Oneness, the wholeness and completeness of the Universe. The magnificence of the Universe flows in and through me now.

Realization: My life flows from the perfection of the Universe. I am an expression of perfection. This knowingness orchestrates fulfillment in my life. I am open to limitless possibilities. I know that opportunities and ideas stream into my life. I am filled with clarity and wholeness. My intention is to experience more of my God Self. I choose to experience abundance and joy, wealth, riches, beauty, peace, harmony, love, understanding, high self-worth, completion, perfection, unlimited happiness, companionship, romance, acknowledge, recognition, friendship, a body weight of......lbs.

There is no molecule of my being that does not support my magnificence. I honor and accept my expansion. I surrender to the Truth of my God Glory. I accept my unification with Universal "Godness" and Goodness.

Thanksgiving: I am grateful and thankful for the stream of good ideas that flow into my experience. I joyfully give thanks as I accept the truth of my magnificence. My life is whole and complete.

Release: I release my word, knowing I have to speak it and it is done. The Laws of Intention and Creation operate freely in my life magnetizing my good to me. And so it is. —AMEN.

Fears Of The Unknown

I, ……… (Your Name), am experiencing new things (a job, relationship, vacation) even though they are scary and unfamiliar.

I, ………, am beginning to believe that I have the courage to face the unknown.

I, ………, want to be satisfied in my life so I am willing to take risks.

I, ………, am taking risks in order to get what I want, even though I am scared.

I, ………, am scared and I have the courage to do what I want.

I, ………, want to say when I retire that I did what I wanted to do.

I, ………, want to be able to say on my dying bed that I really lived.

I, ………, am truly alive when I'm doing what I want to do.

I, ………, am visualizing the way I want my job and/or relationship to be, and I am allowing myself to move on.

Life is the school, love is the lesson
—BUMPER STICKER BY LOVE FIRST, INC.

Our moods, attitudes, and personalities are formed by our perception of reality. The color of the blue sky may be very calming and soothing to some girl who is lying on her back in a warm field of grass, being absorbed by the deep blue yonder. An air traffic controller may not even notice the sky any color at all, as he is panicking about two planes trying to land at the same time. A young child may not even know what the color blue is, and can be looking at the sky and not even see that there is anything there at all.

If I create from the heart everything works;
if from the head, almost nothing works.
—MARC CHAGALL

Where we focus our attention determines what we will experience. However, the essential key to life mastery is being present and open to experiencing each new moment, whatever it brings. Being aware of your body's signals that are always telling you when you are attached or in avoidance of anything. Just being an open vessel to experiencing life, in all its flavors and colors, we let go or needing to always be in control and start to flow with the river. High and low experiences will continuously happen though us. Yet whether we choose to resist the negative or hang on to the positive is what determines our freedom.

Bibliography

Delia Sellers Ministries, Inc., Abundant Living Magazine, P.O. Box 12525, Prescott AZ 86304-2525

Greene, Ida. How To Improve Self-Esteem In The African American Child. PSI Publishers, 2910 Baily Avenue, San Diego, CA 92105.

Greene, Ida. Soft Power Negotiation Skills. PSI Publishers, 2910 Baily Avenue, San Diego, CA 92105.

Science of Mind Magazine, May 1996

Printed in the United States
29578LVS00007B/73-96